OBAMA'S THREAT TO AMERICA AND CHRISTIANITY

By

WILL CLARK

Obama's Threat to America and Christianity

ISBN-13: 978-1508619130
ISBN-10: 1508619131

Published by
Motivation Basics
P.O. Box 6327
Diamondhead, MS 39525
Will01@aol.com

For more information about the author
visit
AuthorsDen.com

QUOTE

"A nation can survive its fools, and even the ambitious. But it cannot survive treason from within. An enemy at the gates is less formidable, for he is known and carries his banner openly. But the traitor moves amongst those within the gate freely, his sly whispers rustling through all the alleys, heard in the very halls of government itself. For the traitor appears not a traitor; he speaks in accents familiar to his victims, and he wears their face and their arguments, he appeals to the baseness that lies deep in the hearts of all men. He rots the soul of a nation, he works secretly and unknown in the night to undermine the pillars of the city, he infects the body politic so that it can no longer resist. A murderer is less to fear. The traitor is the plague." *Marcus Tullius Cicero, 58 B.C. Speech in the Roman Senate*

Contents

Introduction

This writing contains 25 articles that express my concern about the danger Barack Obama's actions and tendencies pose to the security and comfort of the country many of us love and respect so deeply: the United States of America. I believe his actions and tendencies pose threats of which many American citizens are not aware.

At the time of this writing, I am 76 years old. I have lived through many good and prosperous times of our great nation, and as most American citizens I have experienced many positive feelings and many negative feelings regarding the changing leaders throughout the years. I have also experienced my share of trials and hardships. During those trying times; however, I never lost my faith in the leader of our great nation, and I was never encouraged by that leader to lose faith in myself.

For example, in 1966-67 I was in Saigon, Vietnam serving my country in that war. Although I disagreed with the purpose for having to serve there, and I disagreed with the president's decisions during that time, I never thought the president wasn't trying to make the best decisions he could for our great nation. Although I felt his major decisions were wrong, I never questioned his honor or his intentions to do what was right for America.

Another example was George Bush's decision to invade Iraq. There was no reason to do that; especially until it was clearly proven that Sadam Hussein had those weapons - and planned to use them against the United States. Most knowledgeable people understood his indications of having 'weapons of mass destruction' was only a bluff tactic by Sadam to keep Iran at bay. Iran was his greatest threat, not the United States. When Sadam was toppled, that unleashed Iran to divert their attention from Sadam and focus on creating havoc on the rest of the world - with their plans to build nuclear bombs designed specifically to obliterate Israel.

When were the best and highest feelings created during my earlier times? There were two that stood out far above all the others. The first occurred when I was only six years old. That's when WWII ended, our soldiers came home, and there was nothing but wild exuberance about the strength of our nation, the love of God that guided and preserved us through a most perilous time, and the wonderful and prosperous future everyone anticipated. Although I was only six at that time, I can still picture the front page of the newspaper that said, 'WAR ENDS.' It was the top half of the whole page.

The second greatest moment when all Americans came together with pride, with that same exuberant outlook toward the future was when Neil Armstrong stepped onto the moon; the first man to do it. We had beat the Russians. We were one nation united; and at that moment we were not separated by whether one was a Democrat or a Republican. We were all proud Americans who had proven that a nation 'under God' and guided by God was greater than any nation guided by atheists, or other ungodly people. We were 'by God' Americans; and we expressed to the whole world that we were proud of it.

Now, things have changed; America is no longer guided by a single bright light of optimism and aspiration. America is no longer guided by a single goal of destiny to exploit the fullest capability of mankind on earth, as was the feeling only a few years ago. Now, we are divided in aspirations, led with an unknown charter, and so insecure within the feelings and anticipations of others that we cannot even express common thoughts or ideologies without guarding our comments within a framework of 'political correctness.' What happened to our unity and our common goal?

Within that aura of uncertainty about ourselves; and the obscured dreams of our future, we elected a president who did not, and does not, share those foundational expectations and dreams for our nation's future. Those were the dreams, expectations and aspirations designed for each of us by our Founding Fathers, those who fought and died for us. Many fought and died to grant us liberty and freedom and an inalienable right to seek personal success and happiness. They gave us personal opportunity unknown by any people before us. They gave us human reality, individual dignity, and hope as free individuals.

How is Barack Obama different from those Founding Fathers, and most presidents before him? He expresses total disdain for those who strive for personal success and happiness. Instead, he advocates equality by devices to spread the wealth around; taking from those who succeed and giving to others who merely wait on the sidelines with their hands extended. He blasphemes and ridicules God; while he exclaims the great virtues of the Muslim faith. Most importantly, he offers no great hope or vision for this great nation to go forward into the future, demonstrating the highest qualities and virtues of humanity. He destroys the purpose for which our nation was founded, under God, through the sacrifices of our patriotic ancestors. He divides and destroys a wonderful humanitarian and historical experiment - The United States of America.

These next 25 articles explore many of Obama's destructive tactics against our nation, and also include many Biblical references to demonstrate the severity and danger of his actions and practices. Most of these articles are from blogs that I posted to my blog site at Authorsden.com over the past year. They have been expanded to give more information and clarity. When you finish reading these articles you will understand why I wrote them and why our nation is in such grave danger.

God bless America.

Article 1

Why Doesn't Root Beer Taste as Good?

M any who read my blogs and other articles might believe I'm a totally negative personality who dwells full-time on politics and worldly situations. I must confess; the future of our great nation led by one who seems totally anti-American does press me with great concern.

I would be more comfortable with an American leader who presented our great nation in a more positive view to the rest of the world, and a leader who is dedicated to lead us - each and every citizen - down a clear path of hope rather than down a wide encumbered trail of mere equality - and who knows where else. If any of his destination aims are clear; they are certainly clearly negative in accordance with the plans of our Founding Fathers and the Constitution they made for us and our future.

Each individual citizen must want to be different and successful and not as Obama so often suggests - equal and standard. In other words, he seems to distribute the aspirations of average and equal rather than the aspiration of 'be all you can be.' That has been the American creed since the idea and the concept of 'Americanism.'

It's clear to me he is totally dedicated to destroying that concept; that ideology that has made us the greatest nation that's ever existed. His vision, his actions and his comments do not display or even suggest we should maintain that ideology for ourselves and for future generations. His activities seem aimed more in the totally opposite direction; equality, fair share, and equal despair for all Americans.

For most of us, our ideologies, conceptualizations, and beliefs are founded on our life journeys and events that happened to us and influenced us along the way. Sometimes those life events sent us soaring into endless skies of delight; sometimes into the darkest pits of despair. Nevertheless, each event made us stronger and more insightful - at least for most of us.

For those of us who had aspirations of success, life evolved in an often crooked and jagged line toward a goal. Nevertheless, we always saw the goal ahead of us and we kept striving in that general direction. For those who lack positive aspirations, life runs in an endless circle with no ending is sight. For them, the concept of a positive goal at the end of hard effort is a scary unknown to even imagine. To them, it's the 'now' that matters. The tragedy is that Obama promises his misguided followers only the 'now.' He has never challenged them, asked them, or guided them to see the goal at the end of the long, hard journey. He promises them 'now.'

When my wife and I married, in 1959, we lived in Biloxi, Mississippi. I was a young airman stationed at Keesler Air Force Base. I was also straight off a 'three-acre cotton patch' in central Mississippi. I probably had the dirtiest job in the Air Force - or anywhere else. I worked in the hospital, at that time before disposable items such as needles, syringes, catheters, rubber gloves, etc. With a push cart, I gathered all those slimy and drippy items from the wards and clinics then washed and sterilized them in giant autoclaves. Could you even imagine cleaning over a thousand hypodermic needles or washing and drying 500 pairs of rubber gloves every day? Thank God I didn't know about hepatitis or I would probably have found it. Anyway, there's a reason for this little story.

I got paid twice a month - I think it was $39 each payday. After we made all our payments, I think rent was $25 - and we moved one time to save $5 - we always had enough left over to splurge for an outing. It was for a mug of frosty root beer at the local 'Frosty' drive-in, which cost ten cents each at that time. Frost ran down the side of those mugs; it was a great and fun adventure; our only great treat twice a month.

But, my wife and I saw only the future, not the 'now.' After many night classes and correspondence courses, I qualified for Air Force Officer Candidate School. During that time, my wife cared for two babies while I worked during the day and went to classes four nights a week. I retired as a major in 1978.

Now my wife and I can choose root beer, wine or even occasionally - champagne.

Why doesn't root beer taste as good as it did in 1960? Why does Obama hide this similar opportunity to deserving American citizens? Does he have his own - a different - agenda? Before America can be at its best and highest, each person must seek and experience the different types of root beer; not be told to idly stand by on the sidelines and wait for their 'fair share' to be given to them. America is fulfilled by 'doing' not by 'waiting.' It's fulfilled by success guided by true aspirations; not by wanting it 'now' without any effort to demonstrate pride and worth.

Article 2

Why Can't Education be Improved?

Serious studies prove that education effectiveness of a child is more often determined by the family and demographic culture of the student than by the school or teacher. In some districts the teacher who helps half the students achieve a passing grade is as effective, or possibly even more so, as one who helps ninety percent of the students achieve a passing grade in another district.

Why doesn't our education system work to perform at its highest expected level or to insure each student is prepared with life's coping skills? Our education system doesn't do what society expects because it's designed *backwards*. The education system has designed itself before society has determined the purpose for education. This is the first of three major weaknesses in our education system. Is the purpose for education:

Social integration?
Basic literacy?
College preparation?
Job preparation?
Cultural assimilation?
Racial integration?
To create jobs for educators?

Society has made teaching a challenge too difficult for many teachers to endure. Consequently, a teacher shortage exists in many locations, making our education system even more ineffective.

Many teachers try to teach while trying to overcome obstacles that discourage them from accomplishing that task. In many public schools a teacher's time is more consumed with trying to maintain discipline and order, and trying to comply with other socially-engineered demands not related to education, than on teaching.

Now, in runaway frequency teachers are being graded, judged, and evaluated by grades their students make on national tests. Good teachers are often criticized and vilified when their students make low grades on those tests, even if they are effective. Teachers are easy targets. Their visible success is more often determined by the location and culture of their students than by their level of ability or training.

Soon the Obama administration will start evaluating teachers like they do police. Perhaps they will soon start proclaiming that teachers must show more sensitivity to certain students, depending upon where they are teaching. Do students need more sensitivity; or do they need more cultural encouragement to understand the meanings of aspirations and success? Is that not a likely purpose for Obama and his administration to be pushing and encouraging the 'Common Core' programs and systems for all schools throughout America? Total federal government control of any social system, especially the education system is most dangerous for future generations of Americans. It's so dangerous that it's one of Saul Alinsky's suggestions to control the population in a move toward socialism and communism.

One of Alinsky's rules specifically addresses education. He writes: "Take control of what people read and listen to – take control of what children learn in school."

Over the past few years Obama and his administration have tried to take over learning at every school in America by trying to implement a standard program called 'Common Core.' Supposedly, the purpose is to insure every student in America is exposed to the same high-level education. This take-over of American education is being refused in many states, but the Obama administration continues to apply pressure on those programs by claiming 'students will not be afforded a credible education.'

Not mentioned in their subtle tactics is the fact that much Islamic indoctrination is included in part of the Common Core curriculum. This article by prophesynewswatch.com on17 Nov. 2014 is only one example of many to demonstrate the subterfuge to influence and indoctrinate students:

"Pamela Geller, author of the book 'Stop the Islamization of America: A Practical Guide to the Resistance,' has reported alarming recent accounts by parents whose children have been bringing home Social Studies homework that introduces them to Islam. Parents are frantic as they discover public schools all over America are indoctrinating students in Islam and Sharia. Geller's book describes and warns of the islamization of the curriculum and the school room. The book was a primer on how to fight the encroaching Islamic supremacism and sharia that is seeking to convert children.

One mother reported that her daughter who is in grade 7 recently asked her to type out her vocabulary words for her Social Studies. The mother became instantly alarmed when the vocabulary included many Islamic terms such as Qur'an, Mosque, Alms, Caliph, Jihad, Sunnis and Shiites. She and her husband spent the next 3 hours reading through their daughter's book and their lives were completely changed that day. One of the chapters was dedicated completely to Islam and the story of Muhammad, with multiple quotes from the Qur'an throughout the chapter.

The book even goes on to say that "...Muhammad revealed the purest version of God's truth" and that Muhammad is the final prophet of God's truth with the most complete version of that truth. Part of the world history and social studies teachings also include the 1,400 year history of jihadi wars, land appropriations, cultural annihilations and enslavements, not to mention the extermination of the entire Jewish Banu Qurayza tribe of Arabia.

Despite the family's protest to their daughter's school, assignments continued to come in, including one in which the students were asked to use information in the textbook to illustrate each of the 5 pillars of Islam. The students had to mention the title of the pillar, draw a picture and use one to two sentences to describe the pillar in their own words, as well as write a word collage of all that is good with Islam.

Yet another shocked parent advised parents to be concerned and check their children's assignments after his own son came for help with an assignment about the one god (Allah) and the Five Pillars of Islam. Most parents have no problem with their child learning about the various cultures around the world and the religions they practice, but for a school to emphasize and actually teach a single religion to children while discouraging the others is what most are up in arms against. Matthew 13:25 rightly says: "But while men slept, his enemy came and sowed tares among the wheat, and went his way."

It has become apparent that the United States public school system curriculum has been hijacked by a Pro-Muslim Common Core platform with frightening ramifications. Children are being forced to say the shahada, and learn the five pillars of Islam. The shahada, which Muslims force Christians to say when they convert, is the Muslim declaration of faith.

Is there a definitive purpose for education? Perhaps not. Perhaps the purpose for education remains transient and designs itself with little or no conscious thought or good effort by those assigned the task of educating. Society acquiesces to the purpose for education, it doesn't plan, and the purpose seems to trail the need by five to ten years. Until there is a clear and definitive purpose for education, and that purpose plastered on billboards all across America, how can education and teachers be fairly evaluated? How can our children have confidence that what they are learning is the right thing to learn?

Article 3

Three Assaults on America

The First Threat: Deadly Terrorism

There are three simultaneous assaults on America to destroy our 'American' way of life. Two approaches are from the Islamists and the other is from the Socialists. These simultaneous attacks have created much confusion and allow no clear target at which to aim our defenses. I will first describe only one of those attacks. It's by the armed Muslims who plan to attack us directly - with deadly force. Each of the other attacks will be discussed separately.

This is an article published on Jan 15, 2015 by ETV NEWS. It was reported in a newsletter from Martin Mawyer, Jan. 15, 2015, from the Christian Action Network:

"In the wake of the horrific slaughter at the Charlie Hebdo magazine office in France, the media is suddenly interested in Islamic "no-go" zones scattered throughout Europe where many Muslims are radicalized into jihadists.

But it's important for Americans to understand that right here in the United States we have real "no-go" zones that have been in existence for decades.

On Wednesday I appeared on the Fox and Friends show to discuss America's Islamic no-go zones with host Brian Kilmeade. I explained that a group of Muslims known as Muslims of America (MOA) has as many as two dozen enclaves scattered around the nation, including in Virginia, California, Georgia, South Carolina and New York.

MOA was founded by a Pakistani cleric, Sheikh Mubarik Gilani, and are also known as Jamaat al Fuqra (community of the impoverished).

Several years ago, when my camera crew attempted to enter one of the enclaves in Red House, Virginia, we were angrily and violently forced to leave. Some of the enclaves, including the ones located in Hancock, N.Y., and York, S.C., have entrances protected by armed guards.

The no-go zones that exist right now in America are even more dangerous than the European ones which are so much in the news today. Throughout the al Fuqra camps in the United States, members conduct weapons training and shooting drills. This doesn't happen in the European no-go zones.

And in the U.S. enclaves, they even receive instruction in guerilla combat, how to strangle an enemy and cut a throat. All of these activities have been captured on video.

They exist in remote, rural, often mountainous regions of America where detection is difficult. When they shoot their guns or conduct drills, there is often no one within earshot to hear.

Al Fuqra was once listed on the State Department's watch list of terror organizations – yet today it operates on dozens of enclaves as independent no-go zones with no interference from the outside world. The camps have their own government, with their own mayors and town councils. And because they are Muslim, they use Islamic Sharia law to govern their day-to-day operations.

Polygamy is also practiced on the camps, according to one former resident who spoke with me. He revealed many alarming things about life on the camps, including the fact that the women and elderly are often beaten for disobeying the community rules. These rules can include something as simple as watching TV.

My new film, "Europe's Last Stand: America's Final Warning," took four years to film and produce. During that time I and a camera crew visited dozens of European nations, interviewed hundreds of European officials, experts, clergy and common folks.

I also had an exclusive interview with the radical cleric Anjem Choudary, who has vowed to fly the flag of Islam over the White House. All of these interviews are included in my new documentary, as well as shocking footage of European riots that broke out while we were filming in Great Britain.

In the film, it is clearly demonstrated that Islamists have nearly fulfilled their plan for taking over Europe, and now they have the United States in the crosshairs."

It's also reported that for several years many aliens from countries other than from Mexico and South America have been infiltrating into the United States across our southern borders - hundreds of them. Some cross directly, but in most cases they cross over after careful planning and preparation. Their normal procedure is to flow into South America, learn the Spanish language then make their crossing. In most cases there is no tracking of them once they cross the border mostly undetected.

Understanding their modus operandi, an appropriate question might be; how many of them are crossing over a terrorist cell members waiting for the signal to make their terror known? Another appropriate question complementing that one might be; what happened to all those weapons lost across the border through our government's magnificent 'Fast and Furious' gun operation?
Was that operation a random act; or was it part of a more serious and long-term operational plan?

The Second Threat: The Muslim Brotherhood's 'Settlement.'

The second attack on the United States and Christians is from a concept called the 'Third Jihad,' often called the 'Silent Jihad.' In this effort, Muslims have a long-range plan to transpose America into a total Islamic country "without firing a single shot." This plan is already active and is far along in its program.

It's from a Muslim Brotherhood plan discovered in 1991, titled, 'An Explanatory Memorandum: On the General Strategic Goal for the Group In North America.' Just take a casual look around and you will see how far they have already progressed in this effort. Many Islamists connected to the Muslim Brotherhood are already in powerful positions in our government - including important advisory positions to the 'President of the United States.' This is how that document (Memorandum) begins:

"An Explanatory Memorandum"
On the General Strategic Goal for the Group In North America 5/22/1991

Contents:

An introduction in explanation
The Concept of Settlement
The Process of Settlement
Comprehensive Settlement Organizations

Subject: A project for an explanatory memorandum for the General Strategic goal for the Group in North America mentioned in the long-term plan.

One: The Memorandum is derived from:

The general strategic goal of the Group in America which was approved by the Shura Council and the Organizational Conference for the year [1987] is "Enablement of Islam in North America, meaning: establishing an effective and a stable Islamic Movement led by the Muslim Brotherhood which adopts Muslims' causes domestically and globally, and which works to expand the observant Muslim base, aims at unifying and directing Muslims' efforts, presents Islam as a civilization alternative, and supports the global Islamic State wherever it is". The priority that is approved by the Shura Council for the work of the Group in its current and former session which is "Settlement". The positive development with the brothers in the Islamic Circle in an attempt to reach a unity of merger. The constant need for thinking and future planning, an attempt to read it and working to "shape" the present to comply and suit the needs and challenges of the future."

This is only a sampling of a long document. The full text may be read online by searching: 'An Explanatory Memorandum.' According to the document, the plan would include these organizations and all others in the United States associated with Islam as part of the 'settlement' plan:

ISNA   ISLAMIC SOCIETY OF NORTH AMERICA
MSA   MUSLIM STUDENTS' ASSOCIATION
MCA   THE MUSLIM COMMUNITIES ASSOCIATION
AMSS   THE ASSOCIATION OF MUSLIM SOCIAL SCIENTISTS
AMSE   THE ASSOCIATION OF MUSLIM SCIENTISTS AND ENGINEERS
IMA   ISLAMIC MEDICAL ASSOCIATION
ITC   ISLAMIC TEACHINC CENTER
NAIT   NORTH AMERICAN ISLAMIC TRUST
FID   FOUNDATION FOR INTERNATIONAL DEVELOMENT
IHC   ISLAMIC HOUSING COOPERATIVE
ICD   ISLAMIC CENTERS DIVISION
ATP   AMERICAN TRUST PUBLICATIONS
AVC   AUDIO-VISUAL CENTER
IBS   ISLAMIC BOOK SERVICE
MBA   MUSLIM BUSINESSMEN ASSOCIATION
MYNA   MUSLIM YOUTH OF NORTH AMERICA
IFC   ISNA FIQH COMMITTEE
IPAC   ISNA POLITICAL AWARENESS COMMITTEE
IED   ISLAMIC EDUCATION DEPARTMENT
MAYA   MUSLIM ARAB YOUTH ASSOCIATION
MISG   MALASIAN ISLAMIC STUDY GROUP

IAP   ISLAMIC ASSOCIATION FOR PALESTINE
UASR   UNITED ASSOCIATION FOR STUDIES AND RESEARCH
OLF   OCCUPIED LAND FUND
MIA   MERCEY INTERNATIONAL ASSOCIATION
ICNA   ISLAMIC CIRCLE OF NORTH AMERICA
BMI   BA1TUL MAL INC
IIIT   INTERNATIONAL INSTITUTE FOR ISLAMIC THOUCHT
IIC   ISLAMIC INFORMATION CENTER

What is Barack Obama's reaction to this clear and present threat? On April 1, 2009, he bowed to Saudi King Abdullah. More recently, he strongly supported Morsi, of the Muslim Brotherhood, as the president of Egypt, refusing to offer support to Egypt when Morsi was overthrown.

He also supports every Muslim activity taking place to integrate Muslim activities within every nook and cranny in America. This is directly in accordance with that Explanatory Memorandum. Just consider how deeply he has already infiltrated high-level Muslims into our government. Only six of Obama's most important Muslim appointments are shown next, but they are typical of his many Muslim appointments to fill those important positions as reported by The 'Investigative Project on Terrorism:

Arif Alikhan – Assistant Secretary for Policy Development for the U.S. Department of Homeland Security. Arif Alikhan played a key role in the removal of the LAPD "Mapping" Plan which involved mapping Muslim communities in an effort to identify potential hotbeds of extremism. LAPD officials said that it was crucial for them to gain a better understanding of isolated parts of the Muslim community because those groups can potentially breed violent extremism.

Alikhan reportedly helped raise funds for Muslim Public Affairs Council (MPAC) that has labeled a deadly anti-U.S. terrorist attack a legitimate operation, referred to terrorists as "freedom fighters" and equated Muslim jihad with the sentiments of American statesman Patrick Henry. He joined MPAC on April 11 for a special fundraiser called "Be the Change" to support what the group calls its innovative leadership development programs.

Mohammed Elibiary – Homeland Security Adviser. According to information reported in an article by the Investigative Project on Terrorism, Mohamed Elibiary has defended Muslim Brotherhood luminary Sayyid Qutb, Ayatollah Khomeini, and radical New York Imam Siraj Wahhaj. He has asserted conspiracy theories, supported terror-related individuals and organizations and accused the government of mounting a war against Islam. Despite all this, he was appointed by Department of Homeland Security (DHS) Secretary Janet Napolitano to the Homeland Security Advisory Council (HSAC**).**

Elibiary is the co-founder, president and CEO of the Freedom and Justice Foundation (F&J)**,** founded in November 2002 "to promote a Centrist Public Policy environment in Texas by coordinating the state level government and interfaith community relations for the organized Texas Muslim community." F&J's nonprofit status was revoked by the IRS in May 2010 for failure to file the requisite 990 forms that would reveal the entity's source of income. Similarly, according to the Texas Comptroller of Public Accounts, F&J has not filed a Texas Franchise Tax Public Information Report.

The North Texas Islamic Council (NTIC), also called the "Texas Islamic Council," is an affiliate organization of F&J. Elibiary is the registered agent for the NTIC, and one of the directors is H. Mustafaa Carroll**,** who is also the executive director of the

Houston chapter of the Council on American-Islamic Relations (CAIR). CAIR is a Muslim Brotherhood-linked group in the U.S. that was formed as part of a Hamas-support network in the U.S. Elibiary was a Fellow in 2008-2009 with the American Muslim Civic Leadership Institute (AMCLI), "housed at the University of Southern California's Center for Religion and Civic Culture (CRCC), which works in partnership with the Prince Alwaleed Bin Talal Center for Muslim Christian Understanding (ACMCU) at Georgetown University." This is the center where Obama had the Christian icon covered with black plywood before he made his speech there in April, 2009.

Elibiary was featured in a CNN piece in December 2009 as a "deradicalizer." He likened the allure of radicalism among American Muslim teens to "at-risk gangbangers, who want to stand up for their community, to address grievances of the global Muslim community more effectively than they've seen the elder generation."

Elibiary has defended Sayyid Qutb, the Islamist ideologue credited with inspiring the Muslim Brotherhood and terrorist groups including al-Qaida. He recommends Qutb's writing as offering "the potential for a strong spiritual rebirth that's truly ecumenical allowing all faiths practiced in America to enrich us and motivate us to serve God better by serving our fellow man more."

Rashad Hussain – Special Envoy to the (OIC) Organization of the Islamic Conference. A Global Muslim Brotherhood Daily Report took a look at Hussain's official biography and found several concerning affiliations. The first is that in October 2000, Hussain spoke at a conference sponsored by the Association of Muslim Social Scientists, which was listed in an internal Muslim Brotherhood document as one of "our organizations and the organizations of our friends," and the Prince Alwaleed Center for Muslim-Christian Understanding of Georgetown University, which receives Saudi funding and is directed by prominent Muslim Brotherhood advocate, John Esposito.

In September 2004, Hussain played a role in the Muslim Students Association's annual conference, which was founded by Muslim Brotherhood in 1963 and is also listed as one the group's fronts in its own documents. Since then, many of its nearly 600 college chapters have engaged in extremism and the group closely collaborates with the other Brotherhood fronts. For example, MSA was part of an umbrella organization called the American Muslim Taskforce that led a campaign against the FBI's use of informants in mosques and accused the agency of anti-Muslim activity. Several Brotherhood affiliates are in this including the Muslim-American Society, the Islamic Circle of North America, the Islamic Society of North America, the Muslim Public Affairs Council and the Council on American-Islamic Relations.

At this conference, Hussain spoke alongside the daughter of Professor Sami Al-Arian, who was convicted of being a key leader of the Palestinian Islamic Jihad terrorist group and later admitted to being a member of the Muslim Brotherhood. Hussain also defended Al-Arian and described his prosecution as being a "politically-motivated persecution."

The network of Brotherhood-affiliated groups has consistently been on his side throughout the entire ordeal and celebrated his release. Interestingly, the story in The Washington Report on Middle East Affairs that quoted Hussain's defense of Al-Arian has been altered since its original publication. A cnsnews article reports that the quote was removed "sometime after October 2007" and that the reporter who wrote the article expressed surprise but said she no longer worked at WRMEA and could not explain the edit.

Last May, Hussain spoke at a conference sponsored by several Brotherhood affiliates, including the Muslim Public Affairs Council, an organization whose extremism has been catalogued in a A series by The Investigative Project on Terrorism and the Council on American-Islamic Relations. The latter was listed by the federal government in 2007 as an 'unindicted co-conspirator' in the terrorism financing trial of The Holy Land Foundation, another Muslim Brotherhood front that was found to be financing Hamas. Its founders are former officials at the Islamic Association of Palestine, a Brotherhood front shut down for supporting Hamas and are said by the FBI to be members of the Brotherhood's Palestine Committee in the United States.

Hussain's view on the cause of terrorism is important to note as it will play a significant role in the Obama Administration's outreach to the Muslim world. He quoted a study that concluded that 'The primary cause of broad-based anger and anti-Americanism is not a clash of civilizations but the perceived effect of U.S. foreign policy in the Muslim world.' In this statement, it appears that he believes that terrorism is the product of opposition to foreign policy, rather than the product of a politico-religious totalitarian ideology, which explains his opposition to terms like "Islamic terrorism."

On the other hand, Hussein does support the use of the term "Hamas terrorists," so he cannot be said to be a supporter of Hamas, which grew out of the Muslim Brotherhood. He has an entire section in his paper titled, 'Discrediting the Terrorist Ideology.' He opposes making democracy promotion a central part of that goal, saying that it can be interpreted as imperialism and an attempt to bring about freedom that enables immorality, but admits that it may be part of the solution. He instead suggests that the government use Muslim voices to argue that Islam forbids acts of terrorism and extremism.

One other important part of his paper is when he proposes that the U.S. build a Muslim coalition "not limited to those who advocate Western-style democracy, and avoid creating a dichotomy between freedom and Islamic society." This would set the stage for a partnership with the Muslim Brotherhood. Rather than focusing on supporting elements that will genuinely argue that democracy is compatible with Islam, his standard for allies is that they just oppose terrorism and extremism. Apparently, those who pursue Sharia Law through other methods do not fit his version of 'extremist.'

Salam al-Marayati – Obama Adviser, founder of Muslim Public Affairs Council and its current executive director. This is an article by the Militant Islam Monitor, on May 11, 2013, regarding al-Marayati:

"Salam Al Marayati, the director of the Muslim Public Affairs Council (MPAC), is scheduled to be on a panel at the upcoming National Homeland Security Conference in June in LA. The panel discussion is about "Public and Private" Partnerships. The program tracks "Interoperability, Information Sharing and Intelligence."

Arif Alikhan ,who was responsible for derailing the LAPD's plans to monitor activities within the Muslim community is also a speaker at the conference, He was appointed as assistant secretary for the Office of Policy Development in Barack Obama's Department of Homeland Security in 2009. According to 'Discover the Networks': MPAC has defended the use of terrorism and Al Marayati said on the radio on 9/11 that Israel could have been behind the attacks." In a November 1997 speech at the University of Pennsylvania, MPAC Co-Founder and Executive Director Salam Al-Marayati steadfastly refused to call Hezbollah a terrorist organization; he justified the existence of Hamas as a political entity and a provider of social programs and "educational operations" and he equated jihad with the sentiments of the American statesman Patrick Henry, whose "Give me liberty or give me death" declaration was, in Al-Marayati's view, "a way of looking at the term 'jihad' from an American perspective."

Al-Marayati will be participating in the NHS conference under the aegis of the Muslim American Homeland Security Congress an Islamist organization which attempts to prevent law enforcement scrutiny of Muslims, deny any Islamic connection to terrorism and hinder government efforts to educate people about the jihadist threat. Among the MAHSC listed board members is the Council on American Islamic Relations (CAIR) a Saudi funded front group for Hamas and an unindicted co-conspirator in the Holyland Foundation Hamas funding trial.

It should come as no surprise that Haroon Azar,the DHS Security Regional Director for Strategic Engagement, has worked with MPAC in the past. Haroon Azar took part in an MPAC teleconference aimed at portraying Muslims as victims of a non existent backlash after the Boston terrorist attacks. Azar is also speaking on the same panel as Al Marayati at the upcoming NHS conference.

To have a documented Islamist leader of a major Muslim organization with known terrorist sympathies and Muslim Brotherhood ties on a panel at a NHS conference is further proof that our security apparatus is being manipulated by and adopting a jihadist perspective while doing everything it can to deny and obscure the threat which radical Islam poses to the security of the United States.

Imam Mohamed Magid – Obama's Sharia Czar, Islamic Society of North America. A PJ Media report on July 5, 2012 gave the following information about Mohamed Magid and his support for other radical Islamists:

"Mohamed Magid is the Obama administration's go-to guy for Muslim outreach and advise on international affairs and counterterrorism. He is a regular visitor to the White House (even when the administration wants to conceal it,) attends important administration speeches on the US Middle East policy at the State Department, he counsels the Department of Justice to criminalize defamation of Islam, he entertains the deputy national security adviser at his DC-area mosque, and he serves on the Department of Homeland Security's Countering Violent Extremism Working Group. He also advises the FBI and many other federal agencies. He has also been profiled by Time Magazine and the Huffington Post has even dubbed him "America's Imam." His ubiquitous presence across the Obama administration undoubtedly makes him the most influential and sought after Muslim authority in the country.

Imam Magid also serves as the president of the Islamic Society of North America (ISNA). In that capacity last weekend he presided over ISNA's "Diversity Forum" held in Dearborn (where Muslim residents were recently video recorded stoning Christian protestors). One of the speakers at the ISNA Diversity Forum was CAIR-Michigan executive director Dawud Walid. Imam Magid even gave a "diversity award" to Walid.

Walid, too, is popular with the Obama administration, taking two taxpayer financed trips overseas on behalf of the State

Department. But just a little over a month ago Dawud Walid gave a sermon at the Islamic Organization of America (IONA) mosque in Warren, Michigan. As noted by an Investigative Project report issued just days after Walid's appearance, during the sermon he asked, "Who are those who incurred the wrath of Allah?" Answering his own question in Arabic, he replied, "They are the Jews, they are the Jews." Walid also took aim his imagined enemies, saying:

> "One of the greatest social ills facing American today is Islamophobia, and anti-Muslim bigotry. And if you trace the organizations and the main advocates and activists in Islamophobia in America, you will see that all those organizations are pro-Israeli occupation organizations and activists."

So not only are the Jews the cursed of Allah, but the Jews are also behind "Islamophobia" — reviving longtime Islamic blood libels. As the Investigative Project report goes on to note Walid has also taken to Twitter to correctly source and affirm Islamic authorities who called for killing Jews.

Imam Magid's endorsement of Walid's outspoken Jew-hatred raises some serious questions about who Obama is getting his advice from, but it does answer some questions about the inspiration for the Obama administration's ongoing "Islamophobia" witchhunt. But handing a "diversity award" to an unashamed Jew-hater doesn't make Dawud Walid a diversity hero. It does, however, say something about Obama's Shariah czar Mohamed Magid."

Eboo Patel – Advisory Council on Faith-Based Neighborhood Partnerships. Named by US News & World Report as one of

America's Best Leaders of 2009, Eboo Patel is the founder and Executive Director of Interfaith Youth Core (IFYC), a Chicago-based institution building the global interfaith youth movement. Author of the award-winning book 'Acts of Faith: The Story of an American Muslim, the Struggle for the Soul of a Generation,' Eboo is also a regular contributor to the Washington Post, National Public Radio and CNN. He is a member of President Obama's Advisory Council of the White House Office of Faith Based and Neighborhood Partnerships, and holds a doctorate in the sociology of religion from Oxford University, where he studied on a Rhodes scholarship.

Although nothing specific has been reported to suggest he has the same Islamic inclinations as the others reported above, his inclusion in Obama's close administration must still be suspect. The idea of a 'global interfaith youth movement' itself could be suspect considering all the other aspects of Islam. Their ultimate goal is to turn everyone into Islamists. And, combine this approach with the global internet connection with all schools - they have the perfect vehicle to begin that insidious project.

Barack Obama and his administration have supported and promoted many of these Islamists under the guise of peace building and inclusion. But is that what's really happening? Let's analyze the organizations these Islamists openly support - especially the ISNA.

The 'Investigative Project on Terrorism' discovered this plan for the silent Islamic Jihad in America. The plan was written in May, 1991, and is titled: 'An Explanatory Memorandum On the General Strategic Goal for the Group In North America.' This plan was discussed in detail in Chapter 7. It details the process of 'settlement.'

"The process of settlement is a "Civilization-Jihadist Process" with all the word means. The Ikhwan must understand that their work in America is a kind of grand Jihad in eliminating and destroying the Western civilization from within and "sabotaging" its miserable house by their hands and the hands of the believers so that it is eliminated and God's religion is made victorious over all other religions. Without this level of understanding, we are not up to this challenge and have not prepared ourselves for Jihad yet. It is a Muslim's destiny to perform Jihad and work wherever he is and wherever he lands until the final hour comes, and there is no escape from that destiny except for those who chose to slack. But, would the slackers and the Mujahedeen be equal."

The document also recommends that all the Muslim related organizations must be organized together under one banner for the common cause, and should work in the same spirit. That common cause is to "destroy America from within." The Islamic Society of North America (ISNA) is probably the most dangerous to our existence as Americans.

Established in 1981 by the Saudi-funded Muslim Students' Association of the U.S. and Canada (MSA), the Islamic Society of North America (ISNA) calls itself the largest Muslim organization on the continent. ISNA was created by MSA with the help of one of Palestanian Islamic Jihad's founding students, Sami Al-Irian. Another noteworthy founding member of ISNA was Mahboob Khan.

Today ISNA's annual conventions draw more attendees, usually over 30,000, more than any other Muslim gathering in the western hemisphere. ISNA's mission is to function as "an association of Muslim organizations and individuals that provides a common platform for presenting Islam, supporting Muslim communities, developing educational, social and outreach programs and fostering good relations with other religious communities, and civic and service organizations."

ISNA focuses heavily on providing Wahhabi   theological indoctrination materials to a large percentage of the mosques in North America. Many of these mosques were recently built with Saudi money and are required, by their Saudi benefactors, to strictly follow the dictates of Wahhabi imams; an edict that affects the tone and content of the sermons given in the mosques, the selection of books and periodicals that may be read in mosque libraries or sold in mosque bookshops, and the policies governing the exclusion or suppression of dissenters from the congregations. Through its affiliate, the North American Islamic Trust, a Saudi government-backed organization created to fund Islamist enterprises in North America, the Saudi-subsidized ISNA reportedly holds the mortgages on 50 to 80 percent of all mosques in the U.S. and Canada. Thus the organization can freely exercise ultimate authority over these houses of worship and their teachings.

Writes Kaukab Siddique, the editor of *'New Trend*,' an Islamic periodical of extremist views that is nonetheless opposed to Wahhabi domination of American Islam: "ISNA controls most mosques in America and thus also controls who will speak at every Friday prayer, and which literature will be distributed there."

Islam scholar Stephen Schwartz describes ISNA as "one of the chief conduits through which the radical Saudi form of Islam passes into the United States."Adds Schwartz, "Our view is that the number of mosques under Wahhabi control actually totals at least 600 out of the official total of 1,200, while, as noted, Shia community leaders endorse the figure of 80 percent Wahhabi control. But we also offer a number of 6,000 mosques overall, including small and diverse congregations of many kinds."

According to Sufi leader Sheikh Muhammad Hisham Kabbani's testimony before a State Department Open Forum on January 7, 1999, extremists have taken over "more than 80 percent of the mosques in the United States. This means that the ideology of extremism has been spread to 80 percent of the Muslim population, mostly the youth and the new generation." Kabbani based his statement on his personal investigation of 114 American mosques. "Ninety of them," he said, "were mostly exposed, and I say exposed, to extreme or radical ideology, based on their speeches, books and board members." This is largely due to the efforts of ISNA.

According to terrorism expert Steven Emerson, ISNA "is a radical group hiding under a false veneer of moderation;" "convenes annual conferences where Islamist militants have been given a platform to incite violence and promote hatred" (for instance, al Qaeda supporter and PLO official Yusuf Al-Qaradhawi was invited to speak at an ISNA conference); has held fundraisers for terrorists (after Hamas leader Mousa Marzook was arrested and eventually deported in 1997, ISNA raised money for his defense); has condemned the U.S. government's post-9/11 seizure of Hamas' and Palestinian Islamic Jihad's financial assets; and publishes a bi-monthly magazine, 'Islamic Horizons,' that "often champions militant Islamist doctrine."

Many more Islamic organizations, almost all in fact, that are aimed at the one goal of a silent Jihad of changing America to Sharia from within. They have all assigned themselves to that charter - and Barack Obama is helping them achieve that goal.

The hard truth is: they could not accomplish that Jihadist goal without Obama's help. Is he helping them destroy the United

States from sheer stupidity, or is he really part of that Jihad, himself? Perhaps he really does understand what he's doing. Or, is he perhaps guided in his relationship with Muslim terrorists by a statement he made in 2007.

On November 21, 2007, then-candidate Obama said on New Hampshire Public Radio that his Muslim experience would make us safer:

"I truly believe that the day I'm inaugurated, not only the country looks at itself differently, but the world looks at America differently. If I'm reaching out to the Muslim world they understand that I've lived in a Muslim country and I may be a Christian, but I also understand their point of view.

My sister is half-Indonesian. I traveled there all the way through my college years. And so I'm intimately concerned with what happens in these countries and the cultures and perspective these folks have. And those are powerful tools for us to be able to reach out to the world. Then I think the world will have confidence that I am listening to them and that our future and our security is tied up with our ability to work with other countries in the world that will ultimately make us safer."

Is Obama delusional, or is he lost in la-la land? The radical Muslim terrorist goal is to destroy us and anyone else who is not or does not convert to Islam. Why does he think his relationship with them, or who he is, will change that dogma? It seems his policies are leaned more to helping the silent jihad infiltrate into our schools, as well as everywhere else, instead of establishing policies to help our school educate our children and help them find a sense of self worth, so they might find personal success, that will help the economy of America, as well as helping them find happiness for themselves.

Does Obama not understand that the ultimate tenant of Islam, radical and non-radical, is to make every person 'remaining' on earth a Muslim? Or does he understand it and is part of that process? Why does he not focus more on American progress, America's future, and the feeling of self worth for every American?

This is the link to that 18-page 'Settlement' document:

http://www.clarionproject.org/Muslim_Brotherhood_Explanato ry_Memorandum

The Third Assault: Socialism:

The first assault described above is the direct terrorist attack to create fear which could limit our constitutional freedoms in America. The second description was to analyze the 'Third Jihad' or the 'Silent Jihad' to 'settle' America into an Islamic nation. There is also a third attack on our constitutional freedoms in America; a movement that is so insidious and subtle that it appears a great new idea to 'make America more fair.' It's the clear and simple assault of socialism.

The movement started well before Obama became president; the movement had already started in the background. The idea of 'fairness' was promulgated so strongly by Obama - and was accepted by so many of his 'Useful Idiots' that he was swept into office with great expectations of a new and more 'fair' America. What was the basis of his agenda? It's a clear agenda that was openly outlined by one who influenced his thinking and his actions; Saul Alinsky. What are his ideas that Obama follows?

Alinsky's important books are: 'Rules for Radicals' and 'Reveille for Radicals.' In the books he explains how to create a social state. According to him there are eight levels of control that must

be obtained before you are able to create a social state. The first
is the most important.

1) Healthcare– Control healthcare and you control the people.
(This was Obama's first and most critical action when he became
president.)

2) Poverty – Increase the poverty level as high as possible, poor
people are easier to control and will not fight back if you are
providing everything for them to live. (Just look how Obama has
created a broader welfare state; welfare, food stamps, special
programs to distribute the wealth. His actions have also
eliminated many good jobs that existed before he became
president.)

3) Debt – Increase the debt to an unsustainable level. That way
you are able to increase taxes, and this will produce more poverty.
(Obama has increased the national debt faster and greater than any
president ever. It's now over 18 trillion dollars - and growing. He
doesn't even discuss the national debt or what to do about it. He
occasionally mentions 'budget deficit' which is not the same as
the national debt.)

4) Gun Control– Remove the ability to defend themselves from
the government. That way you are able to create a police state.
(Obama hasn't taken drastic actions to create gun control - but he
often approaches the subject. If he gains more power, certainly
this will be his first action - in the name of 'security.')

5) Welfare – Take control of every aspect of their lives (Food,
Housing, and Income - mentioned earlier.)

6) Education – Take control of what people read and listen to –
take control of what children learn in school. (Common core and

his new proposals for free 2-year college.)

7) Religion – Remove the belief in the God from the Government and schools. (Obama has already accomplished this.)

8) Class Warfare – Divide the people into the wealthy and the poor. This will cause more discontent and it will be easier to take (Tax) the wealthy with the support of the poor. (Does anyone doubt that he has not already further separated the rich and the poor in our country?)

Alinsky merely simplified Vladimir Lenin's original scheme for world conquest by communism, under Russian rule. Stalin described his converts as "Useful Idiots." The Useful Idiots have destroyed every nation in which they have seized power and control. It is presently happening at an alarming rate in the U.S. According to Alinsky: "It is difficult to free fools from the chains they revere."

In summary, America - 'we' - are being attacked on three fronts. First is the direct Islamic terrorist attacks. Second is the Islamists' plan to take over America by subterfuge and stealth. Third is the movement by highly influential people to transition America into a socialist country instead of a free country.

What can we do to resist these attacks? First, understand these three separate and distinct dangers. Inform others; and when election time comes, vote for a candidate who loves America as it was conceived by our Founding Fathers who created our Constitution to guide our nation into prosperity and a long history of freedom. Our freedom is being undermined by those who promise great things to the 'Useful Idiots.'

Article 4

Are DroneBots Possible?

In my recent futuristic novel 'Death Drones: 2025,' I introduced a combination of drones the tyrannical U.S. government had developed to subdue (frighten, harass, and kill) patriotic citizens still trying to defend rights defined by our U.S. Constitution. Perhaps that same drone concept could work today to fight what's likely to become the greatest threat to our safety and security. At the moment, it seems our greatest threat (other than our current anti-constitutional government tendencies) is from rapidly evolving Islamic terrorism. Perhaps the definition of the drone concept; and then its practical uses should be explained.

In 'Death Drones: 2025,' I describe two types of drones; a mother drone and smaller more agile attack drones. The mother drone is a blimp, a dirigible, kept aloft as blimps are kept aloft. Energy for motion is from solar panels on top. This eliminates the need for massive energy to allow lift. Most energy for an airborne vehicle is consumed to get it airborne and keep it airborne. Even after airborne, the forward motion of an airfoil wing still requires much energy to keep the aircraft airborne while moving forward.

In my novel, this mother ship also has a 'death ray' but that's not required for current events. The mother ship is also an energy resupply station for the little attack DroneBots. I didn't think of the title 'DroneBots' for the book, but I think that's a good descriptive name. The mother drone could remain aloft, or could be sheltered in certain safety zones. While aloft, the underbelly display could be camouflaged with camera sensors from topside. The mother drone could be either manned or unmanned - but would serve as the control station and energy resupply source for the smaller drones; the 'MiniBots.'

The MiniBots would be the attack dogs. The size and the energy consumed from the mother ship would be determined by the assigned mission. For example, to take out one specific terrorist only a very small one would be needed; perhaps carrying only a small weapon equivalent to a hand gun, a battery for fan propulsion, a wireless connection and a camera. The MiniBot would also have solar panels to provide its own energy source.

One of these little devils could silently appear out of nowhere and kill a terrorist in the act of beheading an American or anyone else. Larger MiniBots could carry slightly larger weapons such as automatic rifles or grenade launchers to attack larger groups. Can you imagine the fear terrorists would have wondering if a MiniBot were watching them only a few yards away. Why is that constant threat and fear important? That fear might be our only effective tool. Threats are only a joke to that enemy.

History suggests that no matter what we do, as honor-bound Americans, Islamists will continue their war against each other; the Sunni and the Shiites. The Shiites believe their 'Mahdi' is on earth waiting for them to bring him out from hiding (occultation.) The Sunni are still waiting for him to arrive to 'make the world pure.' They are trying to destroy each other to prove their beliefs. In the meantime, they want to conquer the world for their broader beliefs. It's far better to have the fear of instant death by DroneBots in their minds than by sacrificing so many innocent American lives (boots on the ground) in this never-ending squabble between those two evil factions.

But then - what if our own government becomes tyrannical; more accepting of those Islamic ideologies? Would they use those DroneBots against American citizens as is the basis for my novel?

Article 5

Obama's Quotes About Islam

I just came across a list of quotes reported by Joshua Riddle at youngcons.com. The list contains 20 quotes giving Obama's views on Islam and Christianity. According to Riddle, "This is a great list highlighting how radical President Obama is when it comes to Islam and Christianity."

20 Quotes By Barack Obama About Islam and Mohammed:

#1 "The future must not belong to those who slander the Prophet of Islam."

#2 "The sweetest sound I know is the Muslim call to prayer."

#3 "We will convey our deep appreciation for the Islamic faith, which has done so much over the centuries to shape the world — including in my own country."

#4 "As a student of history, I also know civilization's debt to Islam."

#5 "Islam has a proud tradition of tolerance."

#6 "Islam has always been part of America."

#7 "we will encourage more Americans to study in Muslim communities."

#8 "These rituals remind us of the principles that we hold in common, and Islam's role in advancing justice, progress, tolerance, and the dignity of all human beings."

#9 "America and Islam are not exclusive and need not be in competition. Instead, they overlap, and share common principles of justice and progress, tolerance and the dignity of all human beings."

#10 "I made clear that America is not – and never will be – at war with Islam."

#11 "Islam is not part of the problem in combating violent extremism – it is an important part of promoting peace."

#12 "So I have known Islam on three continents before coming to the region where it was first revealed."

#13 "In ancient times and in our times, Muslim communities have been at the forefront of innovation and education."

#14 "Throughout history, Islam has demonstrated through words and deeds the possibilities of religious tolerance and racial equality."

#15 "Ramadan is a celebration of a faith known for great diversity and racial equality."

#16 "The Holy Koran tells us, 'O mankind! We have created you male and a female; and we have made you into nations and tribes so that you may know one another.'"

#17 "I look forward to hosting an Iftar dinner celebrating Ramadan here at the White House later this week, and wish you a blessed month."

#18 "We've seen those results in generations of Muslim immigrants – farmers and factory workers, helping to lay the railroads and build our cities, the Muslim innovators who helped build some of our highest skyscrapers and who helped unlock the secrets of our universe."

#19 "That experience guides my conviction that partnership between America and Islam must be based on what Islam is, not what it isn't. And I consider it part of my responsibility as president of the United States to fight against negative stereotypes of Islam wherever they appear."

#20 "I also know that Islam has always been a part of America's story."

These quotes might suggest two questions. First, can anyone find a quote where Obama has said anything similarly positive about Christianity? And the most important question is: What will Barack Obama do if and when Islamic terrorists begin wreaking havoc on our great nation? Will he defend America; or will he defend and support Islamic terrorists attacking within our homeland? In almost every case and every instance, his comments and actions suggest he will choose the Muslim cause if he has to make a choice.

Article 6

All Americans Must be Armed

What would happen if only a few armed terrorists infiltrated across our southern borders and attacked isolated citizens? What would happen if fear and dire circumstances stymied our transportation system to disrupt distribution of food and other necessities? Should we remain, as our government wants, unarmed and unprepared? Absolutely not.

So, as an ordinary citizen what should we do? We must arm ourselves - and let the terrorists throughout the world know that every citizen is armed and ready to use our weapons against them. If and when you are attacked, calling 911 might be too late to protect you and your family. It wouldn't take that long for a Muslim terrorist to either shoot you and your family with an AK-47, or cut your head off with a big knife. Being armed and letting the world know you are well armed will likely prevent that attack altogether.

As you prepare, please know that Obama and his administration are against the arming of private citizens. (Why?) Most certainly, every gun being purchased and every ammunition sale is now recorded at the NSA center in Bluffdale, Utah. Plus, in many cases the sale of ammunition is already being allocated. This new NSA center has the capability to monitor everything every citizen on EARTH does, buys or says for the next 20 years!

If and when terrorist attacks occur, what will likely be Obama's first reaction? To stop the sale of private weapons and ammunition, and confiscate those from gun owners to 'prevent the spread of terrorism.' From an act of desperation - and one might suspect cooperation with a greater goal of the Muslim Brotherhood - those patriots trying to defend America and freedom might be the very ones listed as 'terrorists' by our government.

Homeland Security has already suggested veterans returning from wars are vulnerable to being coaxed into becoming domestic terrorists. Also, many in our government have labeled Tea Party members as 'anarchists' and 'terrorists.' If we are attacked by real Islamic terrorists would Barack Obama and his administration take action against these two groups by suggesting they were part of the actual terrorists. At minimum, they certainly would not be allowed to own weapons or ammunition to defend themselves.

What would happen to unarmed citizens if only one or two Islamic terrorists blocked a major highway on a long stretch with no exits, and began walking along that highway shooting or beheading every person in every automobile? If citizens were not armed, that slaughter could continue until enough armed police arrived. How long would that take? Imagine the fear and horror.

Now, this is the pertinent and life-saving question - and the reason every competent U.S. citizen must be armed. Would terrorists even attempt such an action if they knew or suspected most of those people in the automobiles were armed and prepared to shoot them? I think not.

In this dangerous world threatened by ungodly Islamic terrorists - and others, we must be armed. Our government must not be allowed to prevent us from getting our weapons of defense - and they must not be allowed to confiscate them under any pretenses - none whatsoever under any circumstances.

One of those pretenses is the claim that many 'anarchist citizens' are hoarding guns and ammunition to defend themselves against a tyrannical government. They consider the 'preppers' part of those anarchists. In reality, even the preppers know they could not defend themselves against our government forces. That is totally out of the question and an unreasonable consideration.

The preppers are positioning to defend themselves and their families against two aggressive possibilities. One is against radical Islamic terrorists who might invade their area. The other threat they try to guard against are the roving bands of marauders who might be reactionary to an oppressive government's actions against common citizens. These marauders would be seeking food and other survival items if and when disenfranchised by the government. Preppers' actions are purely to defend and protect themselves and their families - not to participate in revolution against the government. But - this will be the logical excuse the government will employ when they try to confiscate those weapons - and eventually the gun-haters will.

What can we common citizens do, at this time, to protect ourselves and America? The most urgent action we must take is to make every candidate running in the upcoming election declare, without equivocation or evasion, if they support the unimpeded right for every American to own a personal defensive weapon. Those who say, or suggest 'NO' should be voted out of office or never be allowed to enter an office responsible for our safety and security - period.

More information about the NSA center can be found at this link:

http://www.theblaze.com/stories/2013/07/01/seven-stats-to-kno w-about-nsas-utah-data-center-as-it-nears-completion/

Article 7

Mispeak and Gobbledegook

Obama's 'Ministry of Truth' expands. This is a quick analysis of the current events in the case of Jonathan Gruber claiming that American voters are stupid - and that lack of transparency is a huge political advantage. Obama and others supporting him continue to use 'Mispeak' and 'Doublespeak' as described by George Orwell to discredit Gruber's claim. Below are three excerpts that identify some of that 'Doublespeak.' For those who don't remember, Orwell was the author who introduced the concept of Big Brother.

1. From whio.com by Madison Burke:

President Barack Obama is distancing himself from a controversial comment made by a former consultant on health care reform. For weeks, conservative press have played and replayed the sound bite, made more than a year ago by Jonathan Gruber, who served as a consultant during the drafting of the Affordable Care Act.

JONATHAN GRUBER: "Lack of transparency is a huge political advantage. And basically, call it the 'stupidity of the American voter' or whatever, but basically that was really, really critical to getting the thing to pass."

And backlash like this followed: MEGYN KELLY VIA FOX NEWS: "Now you have one of the critical architects of the entire law ... saying it outright, on camera, that they had to deceive people because they were too stupid."

But during a news conference in Australia Saturday, the president tried to put the comment in perspective. Obama said, "The fact that an adviser who was never on our staff expressed an opinion that I completely disagree with in terms of the voters is not a reflection on the actual process that was run." While it's true that Gruber was technically never part of Obama's staff, Politico pointed to White House records showing the consultant visited the White House a dozen times between 2009 and this year.

Now - to demonstrate Obama's cleaver use of 'Doublespeak' regarding his lies supporting that bill at the same time Gruber was boasting about the stupidity of voters in several committees. Obama said something to the effect that his statements were not lies - only that the situation had changed. Mispeak! Doublespeak! George Orwell had already identified it and described it.

2. From hotair.com by Noah Rothman: "Gruber-gate gets to Obama: 'No, I did not' mislead Americans.'"

All the president's men could not shield the commander-in-chief from fallout surrounding recently uncovered comments made by Obamacare architect Jonathan Gruber. The health policy and implementation expert who worked closely on the Affordable Care Act and the Massachusetts health care reform law has backed the administration into a corner after it was revealed he repeatedly celebrated the misleading way in which the law was crafted and the "stupidity" of the American voter over whose eyes the wool was pulled.

"The fact that an adviser who was never on our staff expressed an opinion that I completely disagree with in terms of the voters is not a reflection on the actual process that was run," Obama told reporters in Australia where he is attending a G-20 summit. When asked directly if he or his administration had, as Gruber insisted, intentionally misled the public and oversight organizations like the Congressional Budget Office when they crafted the Accordable Care Act, Obama's reply was terse and direct. "No," he said. "I did not." (Mispeak again. He didn't say his administration was not involved - only that "I did not.")

Obama was joined on Sunday by Health and Human Services Sec. Sylvia Burwell who appeared on Meet the Press to distance herself and the administration from Gruber. "I have to start with how fundamentally I disagree with his comments about the bill and about the American people," she began emphatically. (Notice she didn't say his comments were not true - only that she disagreed - 'Doublespeak!'

Neither the secretary nor Obama addressed Gruber's charge directly because it is impossible to deny its accuracy.

3. Nancy Pelosi also an integral part of 'Doublespeak.'

Politifact.com: In response to a question in a Nov. 13 press conference, Pelosi told the reporter, "Well, you gave an interesting set of observations, but one that you skipped is Mr. Gruber's comments were a year old, and he has backtracked from most of them. He's not even advocating the position that he was at some conference. So I don't know who he is. He didn't help write our bill. With all due respect to your question, you have a person who wasn't writing our bill, commenting on what was going on when we were writing our bill, who has withdrawn some of the statements that he made. So let's put him aside." (Mispeak - this didn't answer the question, or any question. It was what we normally call 'gobbledegook.' Maybe that's the modern word for 'Mispeak' or 'Doublespeak.'

Who can we trust to lead our great nation? Certainly not those gifted with instant 'gobbledegook.'

Article 8

Big Brother Rising

Although the concept of Big Brother has been glibly scoffed at for decades, the idea has never totally disappeared. It's lingered as a threat possibility of the future, but always as one of those impossible probabilities. Perhaps the idea of someone taking over total control of a modern nation is not an idea as alien as first believed. Many signs suggest that near possibility. But, what could create an environment that would support that foreign possibility?

Perhaps George Orwell gave the answer to this question when he wrote that book. Under a section of the book titled, 'Ignorance is Strength' he described how some people use the 'ignorant' to support their own aims. In his book, he wrote:

"Throughout recorded time, and probably since the end of the Neolithic Age, there have been three kinds of people in the world, the High, the Middle, and the Low. They have been subdivided in many ways, they have borne countless different names, and their relative numbers, as well as their attitude toward one another, have varied from age to age; but the essential structure of society has never altered. Even after enormous upheavals and seemingly irrevocable changes, the same pattern has always reasserted itself, just as a gyroscope will always return to equilibrium however far it is pushed one way or the other." After a change in his story, he continues:

"The aims of these three groups are entirely irreconcilable. The aim of the High is to remain where they are. The aim of the Middle is to change places with the High. The aim of the Low, when they have an aim - for it is an abiding characteristic of the Low that they are too much crushed by drudgery to be more than intermittently conscious of anything outside their daily lives - is to abolish all distinctions and create a society in which all men shall be equal. Thus throughout history a struggle which is the same in its main outlines recurs over and over again.

For long periods the High seem to be securely in power, but sooner or later there always comes a moment when they lose either their belief in themselves, or their capacity to govern efficiently, or both. They are then overthrown by the Middle, who enlist the Low on their side by pretending to them that they are fighting for liberty and justice. As soon as they have reached their objective, the Middle thrust the Low back into their old position of servitude, and themselves become the High."

Presently a new Middle group splits off from one of the other groups, or from both of them, and the struggle begins over again. Of the three groups, only the Low are never even temporarily successful in achieving their aims.

What does this mean for us at this moment in time? Even if Obama's proles, his useful innocents and useful fools, support him to the ends of the earth, they will never see the results they hope to see. **They can't even describe what they would like to see**. They will remain exactly where they are today - or even lower.

Today that crisis is sought by Obama; but what are his chances of ever succeeding to that powerful position to which he so obviously aspires? What if he just misses his mark before he's replaced as president - if he is ever replaced as president?

Clearly, the only reason Obama is rushing to flood the United States with illegal aliens; to take control of our education system through Common Core; and to implement free college for two years, is to create a larger pool of useful innocents to support his agenda - central power. He is running out of time - he must do desperate things in a short time.

Does he have enough time to create that innocent/fool bulge before he loses control over our government; the personal control he increases more each day? Even if he misses his deadline for total control, he will have created dramatic harm to the foundation of our capitalist/democratic society. That condition has been encroaching every year within our government - somewhat even while Republicans are in control. They have no choice if they wish to compete against the Democrats for votes. If the Democrats promise everything free to the innocents and the fools, what choice do the Republicans have but to offer something similar to those waiting only for a handout? That pool of voters grows larger each day, especially under Obama's plan for immigrants.

Obama will have put everything in place for one of his ilk to finish the job of thoroughly implanting socialism. With an artificially planted base to support them, how can they fail? What might happen after that?

Looking at Russia after their 'Bolshevik Revolution' might offer a clue. Even after Russia discovered 'Democracy' they still have not discovered 'Freedom.' One powerful man in one powerful system is still is charge of that nation.

It appears this is Obama's dream - not the 'Dreams of His Father.' After all, he said he still has his 'pen and his phone.' A patriot's interpretation of that statement is that he will disregard the other part of government - Congress. He also said he had many things he would like to do for America, but the "Constitution is in the way." What!

Article 9

Hillary's Association with Alinsky

Would you like to know what's likely to happen to our great nation if Hillary Clinton were to become president? I discovered this article while researching for my new book about 'Useful Idiots.' It's from freebeacon.com, written by Alana Goodman, 9-21-14. I had already recognized Hillary's association with Alinsky earlier, but I was unaware of the extent of that association. This is part of the article. The full article can be read from the link below.

"Previously unpublished correspondence between Hillary Clinton and the late left-wing organizer Saul Alinsky reveals new details about her relationship with the controversial Chicago activist and shed light on her early ideological development.

Clinton met with Alinsky several times in 1968 while writing a Wellesley college thesis about his theory of community organizing.

Clinton's relationship with Alinsky, and her support for his philosophy, continued for several years after she entered Yale law school in 1969, two letters obtained by the Washington Free Beacon show.

The letters obtained by the Free Beacon are part of the archives for the Industrial Areas Foundation, a training center for community organizers founded by Alinsky, which are housed at the University of Texas at Austin.

The letters also suggest that Alinsky, who died in 1972, had a deeper influence on Clinton's early political views than previously known.

A 23-year-old Hillary Clinton was living in Berkeley, California, in the summer of 1971. She was interning at the left-wing law firm Treuhaft, Walker and Burnstein, known for its radical politics and a client roster that included Black Panthers and other militants.

On July 8, 1971, Clinton reached out to Alinsky, then 62, in a letter sent via airmail, paid for with stamps featuring Franklin Delano Roosevelt, and marked "Personal."

"Dear Saul," she began. "When is that new book [Rules for Radicals] coming out—or has it come and I somehow missed the fulfillment of Revelation?"

"I have just had my one-thousandth conversation about Reveille [for Radicals] and need some new material to throw at people," she added, a reference to Alinsky's 1946 book on his theories of community organizing.

Clinton devoted just one paragraph in her memoir Living History to Alinsky, writing that she rejected a job offer from him in 1969 in favor of going to law school. She wrote that she wanted to follow a more conventional path.

However, in the 1971 letter, Clinton assured Alinsky that she had "survived law school, slightly bruised, with my belief in and zest for organizing intact."

"The more I've seen of places like Yale Law School and the people who haunt them, the more convinced I am that we have the serious business and joy of much work ahead—if the commitment to a free and open society is ever going to mean more than eloquence and frustration," wrote Clinton.

According to the letter, Clinton and Alinsky had kept in touch since she entered Yale. The 62-year-old radical had reached out to give her advice on campus activism.

"If I never thanked you for the encouraging words of last spring in the midst of the Yale-Cambodia madness, I do so now," wrote Clinton, who had moderated a campus election to join an anti-war student strike.

She added that she missed their regular conversations, and asked if Alinsky would be able to meet her the next time he was in California.

"I am living in Berkeley and working in Oakland for the summer and would love to see you," Clinton wrote. "Let me know if there is any chance of our getting together."

Clinton's letter reached Alinsky's office while he was on an extended trip to Southeast Asia, where he was helping train community organizers in the Philippines.

But a response letter from Alinsky's secretary suggests that the radical organizer had a deep fondness for Clinton as well.

"Since I know [Alinsky's] feelings about you I took the liberty of opening your letter because I didn't want something urgent to wait for two weeks," Alinsky's long-time secretary, Georgia Harper, wrote to Clinton in a July 13, 1971 letter. "And I'm glad I did."

Harper told Clinton that Alinksy's book Rules for Radicals had been released. She enclosed several reviews of the book.

"Mr. Alinsky will be in San Francisco, staying at the Hilton Inn at the airport on Monday and Tuesday, July 26 and 27," Harper added. "I know he would like to have you call him so that if there is a chance in his schedule maybe you can get together."

http://freebeacon.com/politics/the-hillary-letters/

Article 10

Millionaires and Billionaires

Obama and his close association of useful idiots condemn 'millionaires and billionaires' as cheating and abusing the poor and middle class. How much of their personal millions would they part with to help you or anyone else? If you asked either of them for a dollar or a hundred dollars, do you think they would give it to you? Are there any examples, whatsoever, where they have given part of their millions to help anyone - only one single individual? Yet, their useful idiots guiding their legions of useful innocents follow their every word as if it were meant for their personal financial salvation. They proclaim 'financial equality' and 'share the wealth' are the new salvations. Do his useful idiots really consider Obama the new 'Messiah?'

If all the money in the United States were equally divided, every person would be poor - and would likely even owe the government money. Now that Obama has driven our national debt to over 18 trillion dollars, each person in the United States owes about $60,000 each to those lenders. They owed only about $30,000 each when Obama became president. No one would have enough money to build businesses and create jobs.

In that case, should those brave and bold people who risked their money to start a small business that might grow into a large business be penalized to keep everyone equal? If that were the case, then there would be only a destitute and bleak future for the United States. That's what Obama and Hillary Clinton are suggesting we have in America. And, what's worse is that their useful idiots fully support them without even one question of the outcome. If they continue to borrow at the rate they are, and plan, your children and grandchildren will owe much, much more than that $60,000. America will fall into total destitution and despair. This will be the results of those proposals from those on the extreme Left.

Saul Alinsky proposed the 'status quo' of capitalism in America should be destroyed. He didn't suggest who or what should replace capitalism. Is it anarchy and tyranny of the masses? Neither have Obama or Hillary proposed what should replace that which they are trying to destroy in accordance with Alinsky's ideas. Russia and the other Communist countries are great examples of the most likely outcome of their 'share the wealth' movements.

Obama is getting bolder and more blatant with his movements of 'sharing' the wealth. It seems he plans to spread the wealth around - especially to all the new millions of immigrants he's invited to walk across the border into our great nation. Can anyone at this time propose anything Obama has done to support our Constitution or the hard-working patriots in America?

My new book, 'Obama, Hillary, Saul Alinsky and their Useful Idiots' explains much, much more of the dangers he's causing to our great nation.

Article 11

Work is Part of Salvation

How will the beast, described in the Book of Revelation, gather such a large following that he will go forth 'through peace, conquering?' That answer is partially given in Daniel 11. It begins with Verse 33, "And they that understand among the people shall instruct many: yet they shall fall by the sword, and by flame, by captivity, and by spoil, many days. 34, Now when they shall fall, they shall be holpen with a little help; but many shall cleave to them with flatteries." 35, "...even to the time of the end: because it is yet for a time appointed." 36, And the king shall do according to his will; and he shall exalt himself, and magnify himself above every god, and shall speak marvelous things against the God of gods." 39, Thus shall he do in the most strong holds with a strange god whom he shall acknowledge and increase with glory; and he shall cause them to rule over many, and shall divide the land for gain."

So, how could this happen? How could someone divide the land for his gain? Perhaps an answer is suggested in other references. It begins in Second Thessalonians, Chapter 2. Verse 17 begins, "Comfort your hearts, and stablish you in every good word and work."

This word, 'work' could be interpreted in many ways, but another reference clears up that confusion. The next clarity begins with Chapter 3, Verse 6, "Now we command you, brethren, in the name of our Lord, Jesus Christ, that ye withdraw yourselves from every brother that walk disorderly, and not after the tradition which he received of us. 7, For yourselves know how ye ought to follow us; for we behaved not ourselves disorderly among you; 8, Neither did we eat any man's bread for naught; but wrought with labor and travail night and day, that we might not be chargeable to any of you; 9, Not because we have not power, but to make ourselves an ensample unto you to follow us."

Verse 10 begins a stronger case for work, "For even when we were with you, this we commanded you, that if any would not work, neither should he eat. 11, For we hear that there are some which walk among you disorderly, working not at all, but are busybodies. Verse 12 summarizes their idea, "Now them that are such we command and exhort by our Lord Jesus Christ, that with quietness they work, and eat their own bread."

And, we shouldn't forget First Corinthians 3:7, "So then neither is he that planteth any thing, neither he that watereth; but God that giveth the increase. 8, Now he that planteth and he that watereth are one; and every man shall receive his own reward according to his own labour. 9, For we are labourers together with God; ye are God's husbandry, ye are God's building."

In summary, this explains how one might divide the land for his gain. Barack Obama is a gifted expert in this process. He encourages many not to work, not to prosper, not to fulfill their responsible and biblical tasks by refusing to work for their own bread. He encourages them to be 'disorderly' and wait for others to give them their bread through more taxes that can be aimed at welfare, food stamps, more fatherless babies, and self-imposed total despair.

This 'dividing the land for his gain' eliminates those he casts down to despair from ever finding the Grace and Light of God. By his actions with them, and their ready acceptance of getting something without effort, he condemns their souls to disorder and into the waiting hands of Satan. And, having growing support with increasing followers following his 'great words and blasphemies' what might become the final result of his plans and actions?

Jesus cautioned many times, to all the churches, "He that hath an ear - listen and use that Spirit of Wisdom." Too many refuse to listen, and become those 'Useful Idiots.' They allow an unfaithful leader to beguile their souls from salvation.

Article 12

Thoughts From Revelation

The end times:

I've been reading the Book of Revelation fervently for several months; perhaps as much as two years, trying to interpret some of the meanings of those highly coded words and sentences. My last few articles have been from the results of some of that interpretation.

While reading more as the source for my upcoming book, 'The Seven Spirits' I was surprised to interpret - in my own way - that the Book of Revelation does not describe the end of the world - as many readers fear. It describes some horrible times resulting from plagues, wars, and natural disasters wherein many people will be killed. It also describes a religious war in which that religion led by a 'beast' representing a 'strange' god is finally defeated. After that, some of the last verses describe a new story. It seems many people do not read through to those last verses.

Chapter 21, Verse 24 reads, "And the nations of them which are saved shall walk in the light of it: (referring to the new city of Jerusalem) and the kings of the earth do bring their glory and honour into it." Glory and Honor are two of the seven Spirits. "And the nations of them which are saved" suggests our physical world as we know it will continue.

Chapter 22, Verse 2, "...was the tree of life, which bare twelve manner of fruits, and yielded her fruit every month: and the leaves of the tree were for the healing of the nations." Verse 4 adds, "And they that see his face; and his name shall be in their foreheads." Verse 12 warns, "And, behold, I come quickly; and my reward is with me, to give every man according to his work shall be." Note again that nations still exist, but must be healed. This confirms that our physical world will still exist for mankind to enjoy even greater.

Perhaps the physical world will continue to exist even after the great tribulation and after the Battle of Armageddon, and after God sits on His throne in His New Jerusalem. There is hope for humanity.

In the end, according to the last verses in Revelation , it will be a better world without the presence of that strange god to wreak evil upon the earth. Everyone will live in the Light of those Seven Spirits of God: Power, Strength, Riches, Blessings, Wisdom, Honor, and Glory.

The Rapture:

One point of confusion for the concept of the Rapture comes from Second Thessalonians, Chapter 2: 6-8, "And now ye know what withholdeth that he might be revealed in his time. For the mystery of iniquity doth already work; only he who now letteth will let, until he be taken out of the way, And then shall that Wicked be revealed, whom the Lord shall consume with the spirit of his mouth,"

Some interpret these passages as saying the wicked will be contained until those who let will be taken out of the way. They profess this means that when the Spirit of God is removed from earth, in the Rapture, the antichrist (described as the beast in Revelation) will be free to show his full force and power. As explained above (in my upcoming book) this is incorrect; even the word 'rapture' itself is never mentioned in the Bible. Other references also dispute the 'Rapture' theory.

The most likely and practical basis for "until he be taken out of the way" describes a time when the United States will no longer protect Israel from serious Islamic threats. That could happen when the power of the United States is diminished to the point of not being able to protect Israel, or when the leadership of the United States is so controlled by the beast that it chooses not to protect or support Israel. Even today, the United States is failing more each day to assure that prophetic protection. (Even today, the president continues to downgrade the power of our military.)

This attack on Israel is clearly and precisely described in Revelation. That description is in Chapter 19 and includes verses 11-21. The battle is mentioned earlier in Chapter16:16 and is described as Armageddon. This likely refers to the Jezreel Valley, which is overlooked by Tell Meggido, the basis for the word 'Armageddon. It's located near Mount Carmel in Israel.

First Thessalonians 4: 16-17 also allows some confusion regarding the Rapture. Verse 16 reads, "For the Lord himself shall descend from heaven with a shout, with the voice of the archangel, and with the trump of God: and the dead in Christ shall rise first. 17, "Then we which are alive and remain shall be caught up together with them in the clouds, to meet the Lord in the air; and so shall we ever be with the Lord." Some interpret this as living bodies will meet the 'Lord in the air.' Another reference explains this as 'living souls' not 'living bodies.'

Revelation, Chapter 20: Verses 4 and 5, offer a clearer definition. Verse 4, in part reads, "...I saw the souls of them that were beheaded for the witness of Jesus, and for the word of God, and which had not worshiped the beast, neither his image, neither had received his mark upon their foreheads, or in their hands; and they lived and reigned with Christ a thousand years. 5, "But the rest of the dead lived not again until the thousand years were finished..."

In summary, the first resurrection is for the 'living' souls of those who refuse the 'mark of the beast' described in Revelation, Chapter 13, Verses 16-18. The second resurrection is for all the 'living' souls before and after those who meet the Lord in the clouds for that first resurrection.

In the real world today, not prophetically, which side seems to have more support and encouragement from Obama? Is it Israel - or is it the Islamic world? Perhaps his decision had already been determined when he wrote in his book, 'Audacity of Hope': "I will stand with the Muslims should the political winds shift in an ugly direction."

Article 13

Saul Alinsky's Plan

W ho is Saul Alinsky and what were his plans for guiding radicals toward a social revolution in America? He was a social radical who wrote two books to promote social revolution. Hillary Clinton had several meetings with him to exchange information in her early years. Barack Obama not only endorsed these rules written by Alinsky, he also taught Alinsky's tactics while he was a 'community organizer.' The following information explains further.

Alinsky's important books are: 'Rules for Radicals' and 'Reveille for Radicals.' In the books he explains how to create a social state. According to him there are eight levels of control that must be obtained before you are able to create a social state. The first is the most important.

1. **Healthcare**: Alinsky wrote, "Control healthcare and you control the people.' This is the first attack on the 'establishment."

Isn't it ironic this was also Obama's first and most critical action when he became president. Isn't it also ironic that during her husband's administration, Hillary Clinton tried to have a healthcare law passed that would have served the same purpose - to control the people. Finally, enough 'Useful Idiot' legislators were convinced through many tactics, to vote for his healthcare bill. Now, his Affordable Care Act, also known as Obamacare, will soon cripple our nation financially.

2. **Poverty**: "Increase the poverty level as high as possible, poor people are easier to control and will not fight back if you are providing everything for them to live."

Just look how Obama has created a broader welfare state; welfare, food stamps, special programs to distribute the wealth. There are twice as many people getting food stamps now as when he came into office. The median earnings for American citizens have also gone down $2000 since he became president.

His actions have also eliminated many good jobs that existed before he became president. He has done absolutely nothing - zero - to create or assist in creating more jobs. His healthcare activities and other stringent regulations, especially those regarding 'safeguarding' the planet have resulted in even more job losses; and more people drawing unemployment and disability payments. Without a single doubt, in all arenas, Obama has created more poverty.

3. **Debt**: "Increase the debt to an unsustainable level. That way you are able to increase taxes, and this will produce more poverty."

Obama has increased the national debt faster and greater than any president ever; even faster than all the previous presidents combined. It's now over 18 trillion dollars - and growing. He doesn't even discuss the national debt or what to do about it. He occasionally mentions 'budget deficit' which is not the same as the national debt. He consistently and strongly attempts to increase taxes - especially on wealthy people and corporations. He has never discussed cutting the budget at any source - only spending more to give everyone their 'fair share.'

Politico.com recently made an observation regarding Obama's continuing quest to raise taxes: 'The Robin Hood-style proposal would raise taxes on capital gains and close various breaks for the wealthy in order to finance more generous education, family and retirement benefits for those further down the income ladder.

By ensuring those at the top pay their fair share in taxes, the president's plan responsibly pays for investments we need to help middle-class families," the administration says in a summary. It faces long odds in the Republican-controlled Congress, where lawmakers have bitterly complained about a string of recent tax increases on the wealthy."

4. **Gun Control**: "Remove the ability to defend themselves from the government. That way you are able to create a police state."

This is an article written 12-20-2014 by D.W. Wilber at

Townhall.com. It helps explain Obama's determination to employ this rule to bring the United States under more liberal and socialistic control. His desire for total gun control obviously doesn't consider threats we are under from Islamic terrorists and the determination for our Founding Fathers that we have guns to defend ourselves from threats such as that; as well as tyrannical threats from government itself:

"With just over two years left in the administration of President Barack Obama, and with his promise, some might view it as a threat, to use the powers of his office to make changes he believes are best to move the country towards the vision he and his supporters have for the future of America (that fundamental transformation he told us about), protecting Americans' right to bear arms will be even more important as the Obama Presidency winds down.

The president has made no secret of his interest in enacting more stringent gun control across the board in America. While he smiles and tries to cloak his goals in the guise of a "reasonable approach to gun control", he quietly and behind the scenes schemes with his Attorney General Eric Holder to use whatever tactics they can to achieve as much as they can, with little regard for what the majority of the American people want.

The United Nations Arms Trade Treaty, regulating the international trade in conventional arms, from small arms to battle tanks, combat aircraft and warships, will enter into force on December 24th of this year. The Obama Administration has fully supported this treaty. While it violates the Second Amendment of U.S. Constitution and likely won't be ratified by the Senate and enacted into law in this country, it serves as a symbolic victory for the anti-gun politicians in Washington, D.C.

California Democrat Senator Diane Feinstein continues her efforts to outlaw private ownership of guns, whole-heartedly supported by the Obama Administration. Diverted only temporarily by her attack on the CIA and her release of information about the CIA's enhanced Interrogation program, Feinstein is sure to come back to her gun control efforts, which will be the crowning jewel in her Senate career should she retire after this term in office.

Considering the challenges faced by America, with Islamic terrorists from ISIS threatening to bring their campaign of Jihad butchery to American shores, the most recent cyber-attack orchestrated by North Korea which revealed our nation's vulnerability to attacks against our critical infrastructure, an increasingly bellicose Vladimir Putin and communist Chinese threats of expansion, not to mention the regular threats made by the Iranian mullahs, now certainly isn't the time to disarm the American citizenry.

Yet the Obama Administration and their allies among the Democrats in the House and the Senate continue to argue for strict gun control, and take whatever steps they can to continue moving in that direction. With the UN treaty in effect will some sort of Obama 'executive action' be in the future?

Advocating for enforcing the existing regulations and arguing against the need for additional laws, gun advocacy groups wage an uphill battle against a biased news media, that seems to relish using any acts of gun violence that happen around the country as a bludgeon to beat the NRA and other groups over the head, and to beat the drum once again for stricter gun laws. Stricter laws by the way that will have little if any effect on the random acts of gun violence perpetrated by people who care nothing about the laws currently on the books.

But that doesn't stop the Obama bandwagon from rolling along with their gun control agenda, ignoring the U.S. Constitution and the Second Amendment. More importantly ignoring the threats we face as a nation. Which is why we will need a well regulated citizen militia to help protect this nation in dangerous times, and from a weak and dangerous president determined to leave strict gun control as one of the foundations of his legacy." End of article.

Obama hasn't taken drastic actions to create gun control - but he often approaches the subject. If he gains more power, certainly this will be his first action - in the name of 'security.' Even the Bible warns of this facade of security to create more danger.

First Thessalonians, Chapter 5, Verses 2-3 states, "For yourselves know perfectly that the day of the Lord so cometh as a thief in the night. 3, For when they shall say, Peace and safety; then sudden destruction cometh upon them, as travail upon a woman with child; and they shall not escape."

Any action that reduces gun ownership by American citizens will put our nation at great risk. Not only does the Bible warn us; it's also just common sense not to voluntarily become totally defenseless against harm in any manner.

If every competent American citizen owns a gun, we likely will never have to fire other weapons in our national defense. Every competent American citizen must own a weapon; and know how to use it against anyone who would threaten our security or our promise of the future - period. Anyone running for a political position, no matter how important, must proclaim his or her position on gun control. It's the American thing to do.

Our country must never be defeated by a sign of weakness to

defend ourselves. Private weapons in the hands of good citizens presents a strong sign of our national resolve to be free - period!

5. **Welfare**: "Take control of every aspect of their lives."

This is an article Thenewamerican.com, submitted by Alex Newman on 10 Jan. 2012. It's only one article that explains the growing welfare state in America since Obama became president:

"Fifty years ago this week, President Lyndon Johnson announced the "War on Poverty" during his first State of the Union speech. Under the Obama administration, however — five decades, countless unconstitutional federal welfare programs, and more than $20 trillion later — poverty levels remain largely unchanged even based on official numbers, and dependence on government has reached unprecedented new heights.

In reality, Americans' economic fate is far worse than even bogus government statistics would suggest. Even more troubling is that analysts say the trends look set to accelerate as Washington, D.C., intensifies its failed efforts to supposedly achieve "victory" in the "war" while the Federal Reserve conjures ever greater quantities of currency into existence.

Since Obama took office, 13 million more Americans have become dependent on food stamps, with the numbers now hitting a record 47 million — about a third more than when he was sworn in. In 2007, there were 26 million recipients. Spending on the scheme has more than doubled just since 2008. The explosion of the program, along with other welfare schemes, has resulted in countless commentators and critics labeling Obama "the Food Stamp President."

By 2011, Census Bureau data released last year showed that the number of Americans receiving means-tested federal welfare benefits outnumbered those with year-round full-time jobs. Almost $1 trillion annually goes to the programs, with over 100 million Americans receiving some sort of benefits — not including Social Security, Medicare, or unemployment. Under ObamaCare, with its massive subsidies even for those earning many times more income than the poverty level, dependence is expected to surge even further."

Even with this increased and massive burden on American taxpayers, there seems no end to Obama's insatiable appetite to take more from them to create an even larger welfare system. If he continues, soon less than half the population will be working to provide more 'free stuff' and more 'fair share' to those who refuse to work and contribute to the American dream. They have no dreams; and Obama does not want them to see the wonder of those dreams. If they can be imagined, they might be fulfilled, which would be counter to his designs for America.

6. **Education**: "Take control of what people read and listen to – take control of what children learn in school."

Over the past few years Obama and his administration have tried to take over learning at every school in America by trying to implement a standard program called 'Common Core.' Supposedly, the purpose is to insure every student in America is exposed to the same high-level education. This take-over of American education is being refused in many states, but the Obama administration continues to apply pressure on those programs by claiming 'students will not be afforded a credible education.'

Not mentioned in their subtle tactics is the fact that much Islamic indoctrination is included in part of the Common Core curriculum. This article by prophesynewswatch.com on 17 Nov. 2014 is only one example of many to demonstrate the subterfuge to influence and indoctrinate students:

"Pamela Geller, author of the book 'Stop the Islamization of America: A Practical Guide to the Resistance,' has reported alarming recent accounts by parents whose children have been bringing home Social Studies homework that introduces them to Islam. Parents are frantic as they discover public schools all over America are indoctrinating students in Islam and Sharia. Geller's book describes and warns of the islamization of the curriculum and the school room. The book was a primer on how to fight the encroaching Islamic supremacism and sharia that is seeking to convert children.

One mother reported that her daughter who is in grade 7 recently asked her to type out her vocabulary words for her Social Studies. The mother became instantly alarmed when the vocabulary included many Islamic terms such as Qur'an, Mosque, Alms, Caliph, Jihad, Sunnis and Shiites. She and her husband spent the next 3 hours reading through their daughter's book and their lives were completely changed that day. One of the chapters was dedicated completely to Islam and the story of Muhammad, with multiple quotes from the Qur'an throughout the chapter.

The book even goes on to say that "...Muhammad revealed the purest version of God's truth" and that Muhammad is the final prophet of God's truth with the most complete version of that truth. Part of the world history and social studies teachings also include the 1,400 year history of jihadi wars, land appropriations, cultural annihilations and enslavements, not to mention the extermination of the entire Jewish Banu Qurayza tribe of Arabia.

Despite the family's protest to their daughter's school,

assignments continued to come in, including one in which the students were asked to use information in the textbook to illustrate each of the 5 pillars of Islam. The students had to mention the title of the pillar, draw a picture and use one to two sentences to describe the pillar in their own words, as well as write a word collage of all that is good with Islam.

At their meetings with the teacher and principal to discuss the curriculum, the parents were told these were in line with "state standards" and "Common Core." The teacher defended the book, saying Christianity was discussed in the first two chapters. However, Jesus is mentioned once as a Jewish prophet in the first chapter and the second chapter briefly discusses the division within the Christian Church. The table of contents also reveals that Islam is the dominant religious focus throughout the book. Another Christian mother reported her 12 year old son was forced to write and say the Muslim declaration of faith and write it repeatedly.

Yet another shocked parent advised parents to be concerned and check their children's assignments after his own son came for help with an assignment about the one god (Allah) and the Five Pillars of Islam. Most parents have no problem with their child learning about the various cultures around the world and the religions they practice, but for a school to emphasize and actually teach a single religion to children while discouraging the others is what most are up in arms against. Matthew 13:25 rightly says: "But while men slept, his enemy came and sowed tares among the wheat, and went his way."

It has become apparent that the United States public school system curriculum has been hijacked by a Pro-Muslim Common Core platform with frightening ramifications. Children are being forced to say the shahada, and learn the five pillars of Islam. The

75

shahada, which Muslims force Christians to say when they convert, is the Muslim declaration of faith. The Arabic writing on the black flag of jihad (also known as the al Qaeda flag or ISIS flag) is the shahada."

7. **Religion**: "Remove the belief in their God from the Government and schools."

Obama and his leftist 'Useful Idiots' have already accomplished this. This article from Arizona is just a random sampling of attacks against the Bible and religion. It's titled: 'Bible to be Banned in Arizona Under State Law Forbidding Ethnic Studies' and was written by Tony Hendra:

"The Arizona Book Banning and Burning Board, a division of the Arizona Dept of Education, today outlawed any teaching of, or reference to, the Bible in its schools.

The ABBBB found both "books" of the Bible: the Old Testament and the New, in violation of Arizona's HB2281 (aka the Ethnic Studies Bill) by being "totally biased in favor of the Jews" and teaching the "superiority of the Jewish race."

According to the Board the book's claim that the Jews are God's chosen people specifically violates three of the four main prohibitions of HB2281. The Bible is A. "designed primarily for readers of a particular ethnic group" B. it "advocates ethnic solidarity instead of treating people as individuals" and C. it promotes "resentment towards a race or class of people" in fact dozens of them: the Egyptians whom it accuses of enslaving the Jews, the Babylonians, "hairy men," "scarlet" women, the inhabitants of Sodom and Gomorrah the Medes, the Persians, worshipers of Baal, the Philistines, the Assyrians, the Samaritans, the Hittites, and 143 other tribes.

The Bible does not directly violate a fourth prohibition of HB2281 banning texts that promote the overthrow of the United States government, but the ABBBB noted it frequently urges the Jews to "throw off their chains" and "free themselves from captivity" in "contentious and abusive language similar to that of black and Latino empowerment figures like Frederick Douglass, Toni Morrison and Dora the Explorer."

It further noted that the "hero" of the New Testament, Jesus Christ, talks about "overthrowing the law" saying "I come with a sword" and uses anti-family rhetoric by urging his followers to "leave your parents and follow me." He advocates extra-marital sex - "love your neighbor as yourself" - and incest: "I say unto you love your brother". He also attacks members of the financial sector doing business in Jerusalem's temple in a manner "worthy of the anti-American anti-capitalist rabble of Occupy Wall Street."

While HB2281 deals only with issues of ethnicity not sexual orientation, the Board were unanimous that Jesus' sexual profile – he was close to his mother, his only female friend was a prostitute, and his twelve best friends were men – make him a unacceptable role-model for pupils of any grade.

The Chairman of the ABBBB Lulyeta Q. Kukabrskomganivicy of Tombstone, stressed that despite the ban the Bible was still infallible about abortion, communism, gun control, pot, homosexuality and illegal immigration."

8. **Class Warfare**: "Divide the people into the wealthy and the poor. This will cause more discontent and it will be easier to take (Tax) the wealthy with the support of the poor."

Does anyone doubt that Obama has not already further separated the rich and the poor in our country? At every opportunity and at every event and at every speech he makes he rarely misses the opportunity to speak of the 'greedy rich people' and their abuse and disregard of the less fortunate; denying them their 'fair share.' This has been his mantra from the beginning of his first campaign. Not once has he ever encouraged the poor and the unfortunate to improve themselves to take their places among the more fortunate.

His aim is clearly not to improve the status of more American citizens; his aim is to further separate them, their morals, their aspirations, and their effort. In effect, he tells them to sit on the sidelines of life and wait for someone to give them something. This is Obama's most profound act to destroy the principles upon which our great nation was founded.

Alinsky merely simplified Marx's and Lenin's original scheme for world conquest by communism, under Russian rule. Stalin described his converts as "Useful Idiots." The Useful Idiots have destroyed every nation in which they have seized power and control. It's presently happening at an alarming rate in the U.S. According to Alinsky: "It is difficult to free fools from the chains they revere."

In summary, America - 'we' - are being attacked on three fronts. First is the direct Islamic terrorist attacks. Second is the Islamists' plan to take over America by subterfuge and stealth. Third is the movement by highly influential people to transition America into a socialist country instead of a free country. Those leaders simply follow the path Alinsky designed for them. They exploit the useful idiots. Those useful idiots never open their eyes to see a better path. Obama's tactics are taken directly from the teachings of Saul Alinsky.

Article 14

Revelation offers hope - not despair

I've been reading the Book of Revelation fervently for several months; perhaps as much as two years, trying to interpret some of the meanings of those highly coded words and sentences. My last few blogs have been from the results of some of that interpretation. While reading more as the source for my upcoming book, 'The Seven Spirits' I was surprised to interpret - in my own way - that the Book of Revelation does not describe the end of the world - as many readers fear. It describes some horrible times resulting from plagues, wars, and natural disasters wherein many people will be killed. It also describes a religious war in which that religion led by a 'beast' representing a 'strange' god is finally defeated. After that, some of the last verses describe a new story. It seems many people do not read through to those last verses.

Chapter 21, Verse 24 reads, "And the nations of them which are saved shall walk in the light of it: (referring to the new city of Jerusalem) and the kings of the earth do bring their glory and honour into it." Glory and Honor are two of the seven Spirits. "And the nations of them which are saved" suggests our physical world as we know it will continue.

Chapter 22, Verse 2, "...was the tree of life, which bare twelve manner of fruits, and yielded her fruit every month: and the leaves of the tree were for the healing of the nations." Verse 4 adds, "And they that see his face; and his name shall be in their foreheads." Verse 12 warns, "And, behold, I come quickly; and my reward is with me, to give every man according to his work shall be." Note again that nations still exist, but must be healed. This confirms that our physical world will still exist for mankind to enjoy even greater.

Perhaps the physical world will continue to exist even after the great tribulation and after the Battle of Armageddon, and after God sits on His throne in His New Jerusalem. There is hope for humanity.

In the end, according to the last verses in the Bible, it will be a better world without the presence of that strange god to wreak evil upon the earth. Everyone will live in the Light of those Seven Spirits of God: Power, Strength, Riches, Blessings, Wisdom, Honor, and Glory.

Article 15

Two Wings of a Great Eagle

I've started a new book about the war on Christians. It begins: "Is there now a war against Christians? If so, who is waging this war and who are its leaders?"

Yes, there is a clear and definitive war against Christians, and other related religions such as Jewish. This war was prophesied two thousand years ago by the Apostle John as he wrote the Book of Revelation while he was exiled on the island of Patmos. Patmos is still there in its same location just off the coast of Turkey. It's near the ancient city of Ephesus, one of the seven biblical churches, and the location where many of Jesus's disciples taught while that area was called 'Asia Minor.' Although cryptic, Chapter 12 in the Book of Revelation explains the beginning of this war on Christianity and its cause. The numbers below are the verse numbers:

"And there appeared a great wonder in heaven; a woman clothed with the sun, and the moon under her feet, and upon her head a crown of twelve stars.

2. And she being with child cried, travailing in birth, and pained to be delivered.

3. And there appeared another wonder in heaven; and behold a great red dragon, having seven heads and ten horns, and seven crowns upon his heads.

4. And his tail drew the third part of the stars of heaven, and did cast them to the earth: and the dragon stood before the woman which was ready to be delivered, for to devour her child as soon as it was born.

5. And she brought forth a man child, who was to rule all nations with a rod of iron:..

6. And the woman fled into the wilderness, where she hath a place prepared of God,...

7. And there was war in heaven: Michael and his angels fought against the dragon; and the dragon fought and his angels,

8. And prevailed not; neither was their place found any more in heaven.

9. And the great dragon was cast out, that old serpent, called the

Devil, and Satan, which deceiveth the whole world: he was cast out into the earth, and his angels were cast out with him.

13. And when the dragon saw that he was cast unto the earth, he persecuted the woman which brought forth the man child.

14. And to the woman were given two wings of a great eagle, that she might fly into the wilderness, into her place, where she is nourished for a time, and times, and half a time, from the face of the serpent.

17. And the dragon was wroth with the woman, and went to make war with the remnant of her seed, which keep the commandments of God, and have the testimony of Jesus Christ."

A summary: The known world at that time, primarily Rome, knew the Jews were expecting a messiah even before Jesus was born. They waited for him, and at the expected time had all newborn males killed hoping one would be that expected messiah. This mass killing is known as the 'Massacre of the Innocents,' by Herod the Great, the Roman appointed King of the Jews. It included the execution of all young male children in the vicinity of Jerusalem. "upon her head a crown of twelve stars" likely refers to the twelve Jewish tribes at that time.

Verse 14 seems most cryptic until 'two wings of a great eagle' is understood. Jews and Christians were totally persecuted until a 'great eagle' suddenly adopted Christianity as the world religion. Constantine the 'Great' who ruled from 306-337 adopted Christianity after a vision he had in 312 that he attributed to helping him win a great battle against a major enemy. It was the Battle of Milvian Bridge.

According to writings, before the battle Constantine looked into the sun and saw a cross of light, with the words, "in this sign, conquer." He had his men paint a cross on their shields before the battle; that resulted in a major victory. As a result, he adopted Christianity for the Roman Empire. Soon afterwards, his mother made many pilgrimage trips to the Holy Land identifying and preserving special Christian landmarks. This was the beginning of the Roman Catholic Church.

What about the 'two wings of a great eagle?' An eagle with two widespread wings was the standard symbol for the Roman Empire. It was proudly carried on a tall staff ahead of marching troops; including King Constantine.

Article 16

Who Will he Defend?

In Obama's speech last week he stated that ISIS, the Islamic terrorist group in Iraq and Syria, "are not Islamic." Although their stated, and obvious purpose, is to establish a caliphate in the Middle East, which is the dream of Islamists, and then establish a world caliphate. And, since they are also following the plan of Muslims for centuries, how can he say they are not Islamic?

At a U.N. speech Obama also stated "The future must not belong to those who slander Islam."

At another time he accused Christians of "Clinging to their guns and Bibles"

In his book 'Audacity of Hope' he wrote: "I will stand with the Muslims should the political winds shift in an ugly direction." This quote is from page 261 of the paperback edition.

There is also an understanding - if not directive - among Muslims that a good Muslim is one who "does not harm another Muslim by hand or by mouth."

Although his words were spoken and written at different times and places, together they represent a standard question: are Obama's intentions aimed at the best interests of the United States - and citizens of the United States? In his own words he wrote, "I will stand with the Muslims should the political winds shift in an ugly direction." With the rise and threat of ISIS and other terrorist groups have the political winds not already shifted in an ugly direction? Political events today certainly have not shifted in a 'pretty' direction.

As I have written many times, the radical (radical?) Islamic threat we face in the United States, in my opinion, will not come from large military attacks by Islamic forces fighting their way across America, or by bold actions as was the case on 9/11. It will come from scattered small groups or individuals creating isolated havoc - and fear, one of their choice weapons; as in that fear when the Iraqi soldiers dropped their weapons and ran - leaving ISIS fully armed.

As I have also written and pleaded many times - every concerned and competent citizen in the United States MUST own a weapon and know how to use it. All these religious (religious?) zealots understand is a bullet through the head as a force to stop them.

Debating and compromising will not work. They must know that if they set foot on American soil, every - and I mean EVERY - loyal citizen is prepared and willing to kill them without hesitating if they even expose a weapon.

Does Obama have the will and desire to protect American citizens - if they are not Muslim? We must also ask the question; is Obama speaking for himself? Every time I see, hear, or think of Obama, I also think of two words in a popular book: "Deceiver - Blasphemer."

Article 17

Drunken With Blood

P rophesy fulfilled before our eyes: The atrocity of 12 more people being slaughtered by Islamic terrorists in France continues to describe a prophesy and reveal the upcoming position of the beast (the Antichrist) in the Book of Revelation. Chapter 17 describes a 'woman' drunken with the blood of the martyrs of Jesus. Another 'woman' was identified in an earlier chapter as a religion - Christianity. Clearly, this woman in Chapter 17 describes another religion as: "And I saw the woman drunken with the blood of the saints, and with the blood of the martyrs of Jesus:" The term 'saints' in Revelation refers to faithful believers, not declared 'Saints.'

This woman, this religion identified in Chapter 17, can be nothing other than the Muslim religion. Many Muslims continue to be 'drunken with the blood of martyrs of Jesus' all over the world, and it gets worse each year; no matter what Barack Obama says or believes. It's those Muslims who are becoming 'drunken with the blood of martyrs of Jesus.'.

I just saw an article that reported that 4344 Christians were killed for their religion in the year 2014. Approximately 2000 were killed in the year 2013. In 2012 it was only half that number. Unless we take bold action against this Muslim tyranny where will it stop? Will 10,000 Christians be slaughtered this year without serious consequences to those who shield themselves in their religion - and our government gives comfort and support to many of their aims through the Muslim Brotherhood - and political correctness?

We have a president in the White House who continues to support and promote that religion - 'drunken with the blood of martyrs of Jesus.' I wonder what he will be doing in the next few years if he is no longer our self-appointed president?

Article 18

Death Drones: 2025

This is an article reported by Washingtonpost.com It was submitted By Craig Whitlock on November 26, 2014. The title is: 'Near-collisions between drones, airliners surge, new FAA reports show.' The article continues:

"Pilots around the United States have reported a surge in near-collisions and other dangerous encounters with small drones in the past six months at a time when the Federal Aviation Administration is gradually opening the nation's skies to remotely controlled aircraft, according to FAA records.

Since June 1, commercial airlines, private pilots and air-traffic controllers have alerted the FAA to 25 episodes in which small drones came within a few seconds or a few feet of crashing into much larger aircraft, the records show. Many of the close calls occurred during takeoffs and landings at the nation's busiest airports, presenting a new threat to aviation safety after decades of steady improvement in air travel.

Many of the previously unreported incident reports — released Wednesday by the FAA in response to long-standing public-records requests from The Washington Post and other news organizations — occurred near New York and Washington.

The FAA data indicates that drones are posing a much greater hazard to air traffic than previously recognized. Until Wednesday, the FAA had publicly disclosed only one other near-collision between a drone and a passenger aircraft: a March 22 incident involving a US Airways regional airliner near Tallahassee, Fla."

I first saw this article on TV this morning and I immediately had a horrible thought -'What a terrible and practical way for terrorists to commit horrible acts.' I didn't imagine drones used in this manner, but I have written about the danger of drones in the hands of terrorists and others guided by tyranny. That use is clearly described in my book, 'Death Drones: 2025.'

Perhaps the use of drones for terrorism and warfare might evolve before the year 2025. When I wrote that book, I didn't imagine backyard drones improvised to be guided by cell phone cameras and cell phone controllers. There's no doubt - Death Drones:2025 are coming; but it might be before 2025. Let's pray not. Let's hope our leaders are wise enough to have tight controls and limited use - before a disaster can happen.

Article 19

The Mother of Harlots

Continued reading of the Bible's Book of Revelation occasionally offers many answers and clues regarding what some interpret as the 'End Times.' One of those great clues is contained in Chapter 17. In this next scene, one of the angels is showing John another major event. The first 'woman' described before represents Christianity. This scene describes another 'woman' or religion. In my upcoming book, this is part of a chapter describing the Spirit of Strength:

"And there came one of the seven angels which had the seven vials, and talked with me, saying unto me, Come hither; I will shew unto thee the judgement of the great whore that sitteth upon many waters;"

Verse 4 continues: "...a golden cup in her hand full of abominations and filthiness of her fornication:"

Verse 5 adds, "And upon her forehead was a name written, MYSTERY, BABYLON THE GREAT, THE MOTHER OF HARLOTS AND ABOMINATIONS OF THE EARTH."

Verse 6 is clear and indisputable. It describes exactly who the second woman (religion) is - the one that will wage war against Christians and Jews in that final great battle. "And I saw the woman drunken with the blood of the saints, and with the blood of the martyrs of Jesus: and when I saw her, I wondered with great admiration."

The angel was puzzled by John's reaction and acceptance of the woman with 'great admiration.' In the next verse, the angel asked, "And the angel said unto me, Wherefore didst thy marvel? I will tell thee the mystery of the woman, and of the beast that carrieth her, which hath the seven heads and ten horns."

Verse 8 adds: "The beast that thou sawest was, and is not; and shall ascend out of the bottomless pit, and into perdition;..." Verse 11 repeats this identification:

"And the beast that was, and is not, even he is the eighth, and is of the seven, and goeth into perdition."

There is only one religion 'drunken with the martyrs of Jesus.' That religion grows more powerful every day, and beheads more and more Christians, and slaughters innocent children and babies (that abomination); while the leader of our nation - and the recognized leader of the free world - openly supports many of their efforts to gain more power and influence - while he cavorts on the golf course. Once he even returned to his golf game immediately after making a statement about the beheading of an American citizen. How much concern for American citizens does that demonstrate?

Article 20

The Seven Spirits

The Bible Book of Revelation continues to occupy much of my free time. Those who have read my blogs know I refer to it frequently. Probably my most revealing revelation from that research is that relating to the identity of the antichrist, as revealed in Chapter 13, Verse 18. I included that information in one of my recent blogs. That information is also the basis of my newest small book titled, 'Who is the Antichrist.'

I continue to read Revelation, and have read it several more times since my last blog input. One has to read it many times for something to really jump out and create a question that begins to have meaning - at least a point for further more detailed understanding.

The recent question, or puzzle, that's jumped out at me is regarding the 'seven Spirits of God.' Reading casually only once or twice it doesn't seem to have much significance. After reading it many times, I realize that identification must have a greater detailed purpose - and it must be input with a code such as the code that identifies the beast (antichrist) as 666.

The seven Spirits are introduced in Chapter 1, Verse 4, where John writes to the seven churches of Asia (Now Turkey): "Grace be unto you, and peace, from him which is, and which was, and which is to come; and from the seven Spirits which are before his throne."

The letter to Sardis: 3:1, "And unto the angel of the church in

Sardis write; These things saith he that hath the seven Spirits of God, and the seven stars; ..."

Chapter 4, Verse 5: "And out of the throne proceeded lightnings and thunderings and voices; and there were seven lamps of fire burning before the throne, which are the seven Spirits of God."

Chapter 5, Verse 6: "...stood a Lamb as it had been slain, having seven horns and seven eyes, which are the seven Spirits of God sent forth into all the earth." Verse 12 identifies the seven Spirits 'sent forth into all the earth' by inference. They are: 'power, riches, wisdom, strength, honor, glory and blessings.'

My question, and the reason for my further research is, 'if they were sent forth into all the earth, how are we tasked for accepting them or using them?' I'm still reading and trying to assimilate all the references. I'm beginning to believe Revelation is written in a scattered format. Once all the parts are put into their assigned sequences I think it will be easier to interpret. At least that's my approach for now.

.

Article 21

Is Obama Abandoning Israel?

Recently rumors have flown about that Obama is considering sanctions against Israel for continuing to build homes in certain areas of Israel. Obama has asked Israel not to build. There are several reports suggesting this possibility which the administration refuses to deny. This is one of those reports by the Free Beacon:

"Tough on Israel, Weak on Iran:

The Free Beacon points out that the possibility of sanctioning Israel for its ongoing construction sends a signal that the Obama administration is willing to go further in its denunciations of Israel than any previous White House. At the same time, the Obama administration is working hard to relax the existing sanctions leveled against Iran, and to stop Congress from leveling further sanctions.

One senior congressional aide expressed shock about the possibility of sanctions against Israel while talking to the Free Beacon:

"If these reports are true, this would mark a new era of unprecedented hostility from the White House against our strongest ally in the Middle East. It's impossible not to notice the irony of the administration mulling sanctions on Israel while threatening to veto new sanctions against Iran."

"The Obama administration is against sanctions on Iran, but for them on Israel," reiterated Noah Pollak, executive director of the pro-Israel organization Emergency Committee for Israel, to the Free Beacon. "Is [White House deputy national security adviser] Ben Rhodes wearing a green headband to work these days?" End of article.

Obama's disdain for Israel has been easily predictable, obvious - and one might consider it even prophetic. I found his hatred for Israel was so clear during the research for my book, 'Obama's Ring: The Seat of Satan,' that I even gave this warning on the back cover of that book. These are the words on that cover:

"Does Barack Obama's ring carry a sinister message? The claim that his ring carried an Islamic message was debunked when a photo revealed that was not the message on the ring. What that photo revealed was even more sinister than an Islamic message. It revealed a satanic message of biblical importance. Displayed on his ring are two coiled serpents. Many verses in the Bible refer to Satan as a serpent; starting in the Garden of Eden, in Genesis and moving to the church at Pergamos, in Revelation.

This book connects the danger represented in that ring he wears to the danger America faces today due to many of his actions and connections with the Muslim Brotherhood.

Israel, beware the Ring of Satan."

Article 22

Christians Are in Danger

I posted this blog earlier; but with the continuing attack on Christians, and the government's continuing attack on preachers and others limiting and restricting their freedom of speech to teach biblical concepts, I thought I should re-post it occasionally. I believe these attacks on Christians and the Bible will become greater and deeper in favor of the administration's full support of Islamic influence. There comes a time when believers must take a stand. This is only my small and probably insignificant effort:

"In the Bible Book of Revelation, Chapters 2 and 3, John wrote letters to the seven churches of Asia Minor (now Turkey.) I keep reading Revelation over and over, and occasionally something appears just different enough to attract my attention - for another question. I just noticed that the warning information to some of the churches is different from that of the other churches.

To the churches of Thyatira, Sardis, Philadelphia, and Laodicia, John wrote: "He that hath an ear, let him hear what the Spirit saith unto the churches." After reading this many times, I suddenly wondered why this statement was different for the churches at Ephesus, Smyrna, and Pergamos.

He wrote to Ephesus: "He that hath an ear, let him hear what the Spirit saith unto the churches; To him that overcometh will I give to eat of the tree of life, which is in the midst of the paradise of God." There are two clues to this difference. First, Ephesus was the most beautiful city in Asia Minor. Perhaps John was comparing that beauty to the new Jerusalem that was to arrive later, as described in Chapter 22. Verse 2 describes that tree of life in the new Jerusalem: "In the midst of the street of it, and on either side of the river, was there the tree of life, which bare twelve manner of fruits, and yielded her fruit every month; and the leaves of the tree was for the healing of the nations."

John wrote to Smyrna: "He that hath an ear, let him hear what the Spirit saith unto the churches; He that overcometh shall not be hurt of the second death." I couldn't find a direct reference to this statement, other than my own interpretation that one must overcome all the worldly temptations and focus on being included in the 'Book of Life.'

John's longest admonition was to the church at Pergamos: "He that hath an ear, let him hear what the Spirit saith unto the churches; To him that overcometh will I give to eat of the hidden manna, and will give him a white stone, and in the stone a new name written, which no man knoweth saving he that receiveth it." In this letter, John also wrote about the faithful martyr, Antipas, white stones, and where Satan's seat is.

Antipas was the leader at the Pergamos church. He was condemned by local leaders who voted with black stones and white stones. More black stones convicted him and he was killed by being burned alive inside a brazen bull. "Where Satan's seat is," refers to the icon of the medical center there. The icon, as still today, is the serpent. In the Bible, Satan is represented by the serpent. Perhaps the "which no man knoweth" suggests that salvation is a personal thing - one can't be saved by others.

But, what about the general statement, "let him hear what the Spirit saith?" Could this mean that preachers, pastors, priests, etc. should speak 'what the Spirit saith' and not only what is politically correct; what is convenient to what the members want to hear; or what is controlled by anti-Christian politicians and leaders? I'll keep reading."

Article 23

Who Did It?

Hmmm! Very interesting. I just went to recover something from my storage drive (D) in my desktop computer and nothing was there - only a totally blank white space. The 20GB hard drive had been about half full. I copied something from there yesterday to put on a new laptop I was processing.

I thought perhaps that hard drive had crashed. I'm a computer repair hobbyist and accustomed to things that happen to a computer. I just repaired ten laptops and sold them on eBay. I realize what should happen to a computer and what should not happen. I was puzzled and thought that drive had crashed. So for a double-check, I transferred some items from drive C to drive D. It transferred to drive D with no problem. It's still there - staring me right in the face. That tells me that drive didn't crash. It's still a good hard drive.

I wonder what happened. Did someone wipe that hard drive clean? If so, they got the wrong drive. All my current stuff is on drive C, which normally is the only hard drive in a computer. Could anybody please clue me in as to whom it might have been? If they were that competent they should have known the difference between drive C and drive D.

Anyway, if someone did that by design it was a total waste for them. I also have copies on flash drives in other locations - nothing any different than what I post here at Authorsden. Hmmm - I wonder who it could have been.

God bless America - and protect American citizens

Article 24

How Far Will Obama Go?

B arack Hussein Obama's determination to 'rule' the United States continues, seemingly now with more zeal and determination. I have written many books and articles the past three years stressing this great danger to our nation. This is another article I discovered in my continuing search for the 'smoking gun' to reveal this man's intentions for our great nation. Deep research into his activities while a 'community organizer gives much of this information, but no one seems to care; they are too enamored by his promises and personality. This is an article by Congresswoman Diane Black, written August 23, 2013 that adds another observation:

"The increasing lawlessness with which President Barack Obama has been acting in his second term is not going unnoticed.

In fact, in a strong rebuke last week to the unilateral actions being taken by the Obama administration, a federal appeals court came down hard on the administration's Nuclear Regulatory Commission by ruling that delaying a decision on a proposed nuclear waste storage facility was in violation of federal law. In the majority opinion, the judges declared that the administration was "simply flouting the law," and that President Obama "may not decline to follow a statute or prohibition simply because of policy objections."

President Obama's fall from grace as the candidate elected to rein in executive power in 2008 is more than tragic – it sets scary new precedents for the behavior of future presidents from either party.

Just take for example how President Obama has selectively enforced his own health care law:

In 2011, the Obama administration unilaterally ended the CLASS Act – a long-term care insurance plan included in ObamaCare that proved to be unworkable. Congress would later pass a repeal of this program, but it still signaled a disturbing beginning to the President's pattern of selectively enforcing his law.

Last month, the President issued a one-year delay on the employer mandate contained in ObamaCare that would force large employers to insure their employees or pay a penalty. When my House Republican colleagues and I moved forward with 35 House Democrats to pass legislation that would codify the delay into law, the President responded by issuing a veto threat on a bill that would have made his actions legally binding.

The President has now unilaterally ignored legal statute and issued a delay on anti-fraud measures within the law. Taxpayers now are at significant risk for fraud and abuse as the President nefariously seeks to push as many people as possible onto ObamaCare subsidies whether they are eligible or not.

And just last week it was reported that the President has delayed provisions of ObamaCare that would limit out-of-pocket health care costs on individuals and families. Just as the President caved to pressure from big business on the employer mandate delay, he has now caved to insurance companies over the best interests of American families.

The Obama administration has even gone so far as to circumvent a GOP amendment to the health care law that would have required members of Congress and their staffs to abide by the same exchange rules as Americans across the country. The Office of Personnel and Management issued a ruling giving Congress the unique ability to participate in the exchanges while still having employer-subsidized premiums.

The precedent these actions set for future administrations should scare all Americans.

At a press conference before the President left town on vacation, he was asked about his decision to pick and choose what parts of the law he enforced. His response was that, "in a normal political environment," he would have contacted the Speaker of the House and asked for help to "tweak" the law. One must wonder what the President considers a "normal" political environment – is it one where his party controls the House and has a super majority in the Senate?

Again, the precedent these actions set for future administrations should scare all Americans. And they should worry the President as well. If President Obama can unilaterally decide which parts of the law he must enforce, what is to prevent the next president, regardless of party, from unilaterally deciding to not enforce these and other laws passed by Congress? And how far is he willing to test Americans' patience with his increasingly imperial presidency?" End of article.

The most dangerous threat - as detailed in my recent books - to a positive future and continuing prosperity for our great nation has just been subdued by the recent election results. The leader of that threat has now been isolated and placed in a corner where he can no longer be shielded from responsibility by a certain Senate leader. How will he react? Will he cooperate positively to advance traditional American optimism and dreams; or will he become a greater surreptitious threat? I don't think it will take much longer for that answer to reveal itself.

He is now making his own immigration laws. What will it be next - confiscation of all private weapons? When that happens, and it's very likely according to his following of Saul Alinsky principles, that will be the fourth step of control. The first three are healthcare, debt, poverty - then gun control. This is according to Alinsky's 'Rules for Radicalism.' Seriously, during my research I learned that Obama was taught Alinsky tactics several weeks in his early years as a 'community organizer.' Understanding this, how could anyone who respects freedom ever support and vote for this man?

Article 25

A Sense of Self Worth

What did Obama mean? Did he say people should be treated differently based on the color of their skin or their ethnicity? This is a quote from CNSNews.com:

"Minority communities typically are subject to more crime," and "they need law enforcement more than anybody," President Obama told ABC's "This Week" with George Stephanopoulos on Sunday.

But the president also said police must be trained in a way that makes them "sensitive to the concerns of minority communities."

What did he really say? He said the police must subordinate standard and fundamental police work when they approach criminals in a minority community. Is he really saying a police officer should disregard his or her own safety to bow to the feelings of the community in which he or she must function - because those people are different? It could mean nothing else. If a police officer ignores standard training and procedures he puts himself or herself in great danger - in any community.

For example, put yourself in the place of that police officer in Ferguson who killed that young black man, now that the information has been released. Would you have stood there asking him to be nice; trying to be "sensitive" to his difference - while he beats your brains out? If an attacker is twice your size - what choice would you make? Would community 'sensitivity' have played any part in the event?

Again, as always - at least four times in the past - Obama blames the white person for the incident. He places no blame on the black person; or worse - the culture he allows to exist for black people. What is the real problem?

The real problem is a cultural-political problem. The people Obama claims should be treated with 'sensitivity' should be treated no differently than anyone else. What many in those communities lack is a feeling of self worth - a condition Obama must maintain to keep his great following. For his future, he can't afford to allow them to develop themselves into a position of understanding, evaluation, community, fellowship and service. In short - he must keep them within a feeling of dependence; not independence. Terms, as in the past; his proles, his 'useful idiots' or his 'useful innocents.'

To improve our nation, to create a safer nation less prone to tyranny, and a more successful nation we don't need more sensitivity training for our police officers and more officials. What our nation needs is more education and real opportunities for all our citizens - especially those who have been disenfranchised by a national leader who tells them they must be given more free stuff, more of their fair share, because they are incapable of doing those things and earning those things for themselves.

We must have more local job training centers in 'sensitive' communities, and more policies not to allow students to drop out of school. No student should be allowed to leave school without either a diploma or a real job skill. We must welcome everyone into our great national family - not say they are unworthy of that welcome and must be treated with 'sensitivity.'

Would Obama do that for them to help them become less 'sensitive' in their communities. Absolutely not! He must keep promising them their 'fair share' so they will never seek or find their own sense of self worth to become a positive contributing part of our total society. Obama needs them to stay right where they are in their current dependent situation. He has great plans for himself in the future.

God bless America - and all those citizens who need help to find their self worth.

Conclusion

W hat does Barack Obama really think of our great nation; our nation that was for so long the beacon that other citizens of the world looked toward for hope and personal aspirations? In his own words, let's let Obama speak for himself through only five speeches he made early in his presidency:

1. April 3, 2009: Strasbourg, France:

"In America, there's a failure to appreciate Europe's leading role in the world. Instead of celebrating your dynamic union and seeking to partner with you to meet common challenges, there have been times where America has shown arrogance and been dismissive, even derisive."

2. April 6, 2009: Ankara, Turkey:

"Another issue that confronts all democracies as they move to the future is how we deal with the past. The United States is still working through some of our own darker periods in our history."

3. April 17, 2009, Port of Spain, Trinidad and Tobago:

"While the United States has done much to promote peace and prosperity in the hemisphere, we have at times been disengaged, and at times we sought to dictate our terms."

4. April 20, 2009: CIA headquarters, Langley, VA:

"Don't be discouraged that we have to acknowledge potentially we've made some mistakes. That's how we learn."

5. May 21, 2009: National Archives in Washington D.C.:

"Unfortunately, faced with an uncertain threat, our government made a series of hasty decisions. ... I also believe that all too often our government made decisions based on fear rather than foresight; that all too often our government trimmed facts and evidence to fit ideological predispositions. Instead of strategically applying our power and our principles, too often we set those principles aside as luxuries that we could no longer afford. And during this season of fear, too many of us — Democrats and Republicans, politicians, journalists, and citizens — fell silent. In other words, we went off course."

Obama's every word regarding America or pertaining to America has been derisive or derogatory. He apologizes for our past, although we have the greatest past that's ever existed; aimed at the great purposes of personal aspirations, salvation, and humanity. He disregards the kindness and accomplishments of our great nation to embellish what he perceives as weaknesses and fallacies. And, on several occasions he even went out of his way to blaspheme and deny our God who has blessed us with our many great gifts.

He claims to be a Christian, but would a Christian equate God with "Bibles and guns?" Or, would a Christian be smug in derisively equating Leviticus with the type of national defense we should choose?

If he is a Christian, why does he invite only Muslim leaders to share White House events with him? He has lied many times before; perhaps this is his greatest lie. Has he also been untruthful about where he plans to lead our great nation? On the other hand, he has never expressed a destiny toward which to lead our great nation. Why not?

Finally, what's the greatest expression Obama could make to show his purpose in office is to lead America to a positive and safe future - as true Americans? He should abandon his expressions of gun control and should encourage every competent citizen to own a weapon and be prepared to use it. The reason has been fully explained throughout this writing. If every competent American citizen is armed against terrorism, we likely will never have to fire a shot in our own defense.

Is Barack Obama a real American citizen? Does he really love this great nation? Let his words and actions speak loudly and clearly, that we might live in peace and understanding

God bless America.

About the Author

Will Clark's author experiences began by writing inspection and evaluation reports in the U.S. Air Force. He is a retired Air Force officer and a Vietnam veteran, serving in Saigon from 1966 to 1967. His other overseas assignments include Misawa, Japan and Ankara, Turkey.

In 1995, he authored a book, *How to Learn*, as a county-wide study skills project to encourage students to improve their grades in DeSoto County, Mississippi. Education supporters printed and distributed four thousand copies. He also wrote a weekly education column for a local newspaper, *The Desoto County Tribune,* the following school year.

His next published book was *School Bells and Broken Tales*, a parody of nursery rhyme characters, also a motivation and education book for children. His other books include *Shades of Retribution*, a historical novel, and *Simply Success*, a motivation guide for students and employees.

His action novels include a trilogy based on Atlantis and crystals. The first book is titled: *The Atlantis Crystal.* The second book is titled: *She Waits In Atlantis*. The third is: *Return to Atlantis*. This trilogy is based on his travels while assigned to Turkey, site of the ancient city of Troy.

His previous political action novel, *666: Mark of the Beast*, is a sequel to another political action novel, *America 20XX: The New World Order.*

Clark and his wife, Marie, live in Diamondhead, Mississippi, where they play golf with many friends.

For more information about the author visit:

http://www.authorsden.com/visit/author.asp?authorid=1496

Things We Must Never Forget
Until We Know All the Answers

Benghazi

Why were four Americans killed?
Where was Hillary Clinton while it was happening?
Where was Barack Obama while it was happening?
Why did they lie and blame the event on a video?
Why were rescuers on 'stand by' told to 'stand down?'

Fast and Furious

Who authorized the operation?
Why did the operation continue after weapons were lost?
Why did the procedure have no procedure?
Why weren't tracking devices used?

The IRS Scandal

What was the highest level involved?
Who initiated it?
Why hasn't anyone been fired or reprimanded?
What dangers could be unleashed by this organization?

Greatest Quotes
of
Our Time

Michelle Obama
February 18, 2008
"For the first time in my adult life I am proud of my country."
(Age 44)

Barack Obama
March 9, 2008
"We are no longer a Christian nation - at least not just."

September 25, 2012
Remarks to the UN General Assembly
"The future must not belong to those who slander Islam."

Nancy Pelosi
March 9, 2010
"We have to pass the bill so that you can find out what is in it."

Hillary Clinton
January 23, 2013
"What difference, at this point, does it make?"

December 3, 2014
"...showing respect even for one's enemies, trying to
understand and insofar as psychologically possible, empathize
with their perspective and point of view."

Other Books by the Author

Novels:
Shades of Retribution
The Atlantis Crystal
She Waits in Atlantis
Return to Atlantis
America 20XX: The New World Order
666: Mark of the Beast
Death Drones: 2025

Children's Books:
Forest Trails and Fairy Tales
Wishing Wells and Broken Tales
Student Study Skills
American Heroes: Students Who Learn

Non-Fiction:
Simply Success
The Education Jungle
How to Learn
The Day America Died
Obama's Ring: The Seat of Satan
Managing Without Conflict
The Peer Pressure Monster
The War on Christians
Who is the Antichrist
The War on Christians
The Seven Spirits
Obama, Hillary, Saul Alinsky and their Useful Idiots